What's Wrong With Socialism

What's Wrong With Socialism

A BIBLICAL EXPLORATION FOR EVERYONE

DANIEL ALAN BRUBAKER

Think and Tell

Love does no wrong to a neighbor; therefore love is the fulfillment of the law.

— ROMANS 13:10

Woe to those who call evil good and good evil, who put darkness for light and light for darkness, who put bitter for sweet and sweet for bitter.

— ISAIAH 5:20

Evil men do not understand justice, but those who seek the LORD understand all things.

— PROVERBS 28:5

Contents

Preface

Much of our world drifts, largely unmoored, on a sea of moral relativism. This situation is not new—it was evident in the question Pontius Pilate asked of Jesus on (I believe) April 3, 33 A.D., "What is truth?"

Every social or political problem is the result of some departure from what God has said is right. While we cannot force perfect justice upon the world, we ought to at least be able to discern good from evil and try to uphold the former. Jesus called His followers salt and light, and those who follow Him should be seasoning the world with goodness. Christians, of all people, should be agreed on matters about which God has spoken clearly, and united in rejection of those things that God calls sin. Such unity need not be purchased with uncritical groupthink or suppression of discussion, reflection, and dissent. God did not make us robots. We can and should test truth claims.

In these pages I ask whether socialism is something anyone can support without sinning. As the book title suggests, I believe the answer is "no." When exception, nuance, or qualification is needed, I trust readers will find that I've added these. I hope to avoid the error, for which I have faulted others, of disingenuously using God's word as a mere prop to support our own preferences. As you read, I invite your active engagement. Do not take my word for any point; check it out for yourself.

I began work on this book nearly a decade ago. I first considered taking a more secular approach, but gradually became convinced that direct theological treatment was most needed, since even some Christians today advocate for evil, calling it good. I've written to capture the gravity of the topic, but not to say everything that could be said. In the future, I may write more.

You and I are sinful people, but we can work toward doing what is right. May we have the courage to do justice and love mercy while remembering the difference. May we not wrong our neighbors. May we ever love what God loves and hate what He hates.

D. B.

Lovettsville, October 2024

Acknowledgments

"In abundance of counselors there is victory" (Proverbs 11:14). I am grateful to each of the following individuals who read portions of this work and offered suggestions for improvement: Avigail Brubaker, Elizabeth Brubaker, Latha Brubaker, Rivka Brubaker, Jon Garber, Steve Heyl, Ed Nix, and Stan Watson. Xi Van Fleet kindly helped with statistics on victims of Communism. Professional proofreading was provided by Leah Garber. These acknowledgments having been made, remaining shortcomings are my own.

Introduction

You are worried. Every day you see your nation becoming more lawless. Masses of people who do not pay taxes are voting themselves more and more benefits and checks, which will be paid for by others who, they suggest, deserve to have it "stuck to" them. Then you hear people—maybe even your pastor or Bible study leader—insisting that because the Bible says we need to love "the least of these," you must support wealth redistribution schemes. In your heart you know these policies are wrong. You sense that the Bible is being misrepresented in its alleged support of socialist programs, but you don't really know how to explain why, much less figure out how to stop this constant march toward socialism.

Imagine a world in which people understand what justice is. A world in which you are confident that no matter whether you are the richest or poorest, born here or somewhere else, of one race or another, society is together committed to striving for real truth and seeing that true justice prevails if you are wronged. There is no bureaucrat with a DEI badge and a chip on her shoulder calculating how much—based upon your race, your sex,

your beliefs, your economic situation, or other factors—
you deserve to be harmed in the name of "social justice."

I have good news for you. It is not news of utopia
filled with perfect peace and justice right beyond the hori-
zon. Since people are sinful, that is a pipe dream. Rather,
it is a promise that by correcting our understanding of
what justice *is*, we can reject false justice and get back on
track to a generally good and unified society that does a
pretty good job of protecting all our neighbors from
abuse.

Here is what you can expect in this book: In Chapter
1, we will define socialism and take a look at what makes it
attractive to some people. But we do not stop there; we
will also make a first presentation of why the shiny
brochure selling socialism to the world is actually a deception. We will peel back the veneer and reveal what lies at
the heart of the socialist worldview and societal structure,
and then conclude with a preview of what people can expect if they transform their society into a socialist
"utopia."

Our next step, in Chapter 2, will be to take a re-
freshing look at what the Bible says about justice and
about mercy—both of them things that God *loves*, but
that are *not the same thing*. If you read nothing more than
this chapter, you will already be well on your way to correcting the error of our time and becoming part of the
solution of restoring true justice in society. Chapter 2 is
long—I saw no way to sensibly divide it—but foundational to what follows.

Books such as John Rawls' *Theory of Justice* (1971),
and documents like the United Nations' *UNDHR*
(1948), and the Catholic *Rerum Novarum* (1891) have
each presented injustice as though it is justice. Since our
world has now become calibrated to these crooked standards, it is critically important that we re-establish a true
measure. Chapter 3 looks at the most defining feature of
justice: It must be the same for everyone, without prefer-

ence for the rich or for the poor, or else it does not exist at all.

Advocates for socialism regularly portray themselves as lovers of the poor and downtrodden, and anyone who opposes socialism as heartless and uncompassionate. We reverse that narrative throughout the book by challenging socialists' claims that they are the ones who really care about the poor. But meanwhile, in Chapter 4, we will take some time to remember just how very much God does care for poor people—and that because He does, so also should we.

Free markets and the affirmation of property, which are just according to a biblical standard, will result in un-equal distribution of wealth—with some people accumu-lating a great quantity. What shall we do, then, with Jesus' command to His disciples not to acquire gold or silver in Matthew 10? Are those who seek to be Jesus' disciples living in sin if we acquire wealth? And do any of us (or government) have a right to be the arbiter of how much wealth our neighbor acquires? Socialists take a position on these questions; in Chapter 5 we will weigh them, as usual, in light of the Bible.

The Ten Commandments are the basis for God's en-tire moral law, just as the great commandment (Matthew 22:35-40) is the basis for the Ten Commandments. We cannot assess justice according to the Bible if we ignore God's laws. And, if socialism is not in alignment with the Ten Commandments, as a most basic benchmark, there is no way it can be considered just. In Chapter 6, we dis-cover one of the main reasons that socialism is unjust: It violates several of the Ten Commandments.

Work is a moral imperative. The fourth command-ment tells us to work for six days each week, following the example of God in His act of creating everything. How does the socialist worldview see work and its fruits, and how does this view fit with what God says? These are the questions we will consider in Chapter 7.

"Wait!" someone will say, "the early church in Acts practiced socialism—actually, those believers practiced *communism*! Isn't that proof that God endorses such a system of common ownership?" In Chapter 8, we look at the Acts church and notice details that reveal that it was actually an *affirmation* of private property and the individual's decision to do with it as he or she sees fit. The Acts church was practicing neither socialism nor communism, and after reading Chapter 8 you will understand why.

Many social and political problems exist because of unquestioned premises. Two unquestioned premises lead to confusion around the questions, "Is it unjust for wealth to be unevenly distributed?" and "Is it unjust for workers to be paid different wages for the same job?" Jesus' answer may surprise you. In Chapter 9 we look at one of the clearest biblical affirmations that private property, free markets, contracts, and the right of people to set wages at different levels by mutual agreement are all *just*.

But what about when Jesus said that the person with two tunics should give one to the person who has none? Isn't that a clear endorsement of equal outcomes, of the contention that property should be leveled out between everyone? First, it was John the Baptist, not Jesus, who said that. And second, no, John was not endorsing forced wealth redistribution. These facts will become clear as we consider the details of the passage in Chapter 10.

As we will have already established in Chapter 4, God loves the poor and we should too. What does loving the poor look like in real life? Socialism purports to provide an answer—an answer that by now readers should see is fatally flawed. John's instructions discussed in Chapter 10 constitute one righteous imperative to provide for neighbors in desperate need. In Chapter 11 we encounter God's earlier instruction that landowners should leave the edges of their fields unharvested—another just provision for the poor that, like all of God's designs on these matters, does not subject property owners to injustice.

Just as Abraham and Sarah in Canaan, and later the sons of Jacob in Egypt, found themselves to be strangers in a strange land, so we all are merely visitors on this earth, living here for a little while. Humbly recognizing that fact, while also reflecting God's love for others in our lives, means remembering what it was like for us to be strangers in need. What does it mean for us to welcome the stranger, and how does this work in real situations? Does welcoming the stranger mean ignoring the laws of the land? No, according to the Bible, it does not, and this matter will be considered in Chapter 12.

The disposition of goods and services by the owner through free exchange (buying and selling) is one of the most basic principles that recurs in the Bible. For justice to exist in these circumstances, several things must be affirmed, including *ownership* of property and labor, the *justice* of the agreement between buyer and seller, the use of *honest weights and measures*, and the enforcement of the terms of whatever arrangement is agreed. These matters are discussed in Chapter 13.

When God's people entered the Promised Land, He commanded them to return fields and other real estate to the original owner—the person to whom it was first assigned, or to his heirs—every fiftieth year. In Chapter 14 we will discuss this system and other rules associated with the sabbatical years and the year of Jubilee—and what, if anything, they have to teach us in our examination of socialism.

Slavery has existed in various forms throughout human history. When slavery is involuntary (that is, not chosen), it is generally unjust. Many people, however, who recognize that involuntary servitude is wrong fail to understand that democratic socialism is a form of involuntary servitude in which some people use their vote to force other people to work for them against their will.

Discussing this important matter and measuring it against what God says is just will be our task in Chapter 15.

Sometimes, people who do not know God's word will show their ignorance by picking out a familiar biblical phrase and totally misapplying it by failing to notice how it is referenced in scripture. In Chapter 16, we will consider one such phrase, the term "my brother's keeper." We will learn that nowhere in the Bible does God say that being our brother's keeper is a good thing.

How do you spot a liar? One way dishonesty comes to light is when the story starts to break down or be exposed through inconsistencies when the principles are applied. In Chapter 17, we will compare how the socialist philosophy falls under its own weight and is incoherent in its assessment of human nature by supposing that it will be different based upon the position in society a person occupies. In this chapter, we will also review why the system that we call capitalism is a basic embodiment of biblical justice in the area of human economic relationships.

In Chapter 18, we will revisit and expand upon the reasons that socialism is attractive to some people, first mentioned in Chapter 1, to conclude the main part of the book with a short review of the several types of people who want socialism in the world today. This presentation will help us understand and have compassion for these neighbors, and also (by seeing their motivations) to be better prepared to resist their prescriptions for society while still loving them as human beings made in the image of God.

"Love must be without hypocrisy," we are told in Romans 12:9, which continues, "Abhor what is evil; cling to what is good." We have already seen several times that the entire Law and Prophets can be summed up in the command to love God, with the second greatest commandment being to love our neighbor as ourself. Chapter 19 draws the conclusion: Loving our neighbor and loving God is not compatible with support for democratic socialism. Can a Christian advocate for socialism? Yes, but generally not without sinning against God.

The Appendix contains a brief history and analysis of liberation theology, one of the vehicles by which Marxists have infiltrated and hijacked many undiscerning Christian churches.

* * *

I am a Christian who has read my Bible. I am also an academic with a PhD in Religious Studies from Rice University (2014). Such academic study leads some Christians to lose their faith. Not so with me. My foundation was laid over years, including as a student in Cell and Molecular Biology at the University of Washington, next as a working husband supporting my wife through medical school, and then as a doctoral student in the early history of the Quran—all while remaining involved variously as an elder, treasurer, worship leader, Sunday School teacher, professor, Gideon, and author serving our local church, wherever we happened to be.

There are two more items relevant to my qualifications to write this book. The first is that I am a careful writer. The second is the fact that throughout my adult life I've tried to keep my political understandings in alignment with the Bible, while also applying this moral anchor to the big political questions of our day. From this exercise alone, I have a certain moral sense, and healthy zeal, that I hope will be a benefit to you.

I conclude this introduction with two challenges. First, please read this book right through to the end—and have fun doing so. And second, James 1:22-25 reminds us,

> But prove yourselves doers of the word, and not merely
> hearers who delude themselves. For if anyone is a hearer
> of the word and not a doer, he is like a man who looks

at his natural face in a mirror; for *once* he has looked at himself and gone away, he has immediately forgotten what kind of person he was. But one who looks intently at the perfect law, the *law* of liberty, and abides by it, not having become a forgetful hearer but an effectual doer, this man will be blessed in what he does.

In the pages to follow, may you come face to face with the mirror of God's word—even if you are not yet a Christian. In His word may you reflect upon your own image, and then go and apply these lessons in order to establish true justice and genuine mercy for the sake of all our neighbors in this generation.

CHAPTER 1

What is Socialism?

"It's just a standard contract; no need to read the fine print," says the used car salesman, as he smiles ear to ear. His eyes are so sincere, and you find yourself thinking, "This man wouldn't lead me wrong; he really cares about me."

The huckster has sized you up as a sucker and sees an opportunity to unload a lemon. He avoids mentioning the car's problems. He distracts, sets you at ease with smooth words, and pushes to conclude the sale fast, before you have time to catch on to what is happening.

Socialism gains traction the same way. Like the shiny set of wheels that caught your eye in the car lot, so also socialism makes a nice first impression. But since it is not self-evidently good on examination, its advocates deploy slick salesmanship and smooth public relations campaigns to win over a critical mass of the voting public.

This book is about socialism. But what does that word mean? What is socialism, what does it do, and how does it work? Most importantly, what effect does it have on real people who live under it?

The word *socialism* was coined in England in the

1820s.[1] Socialism is a name for a family of economic systems that deny the existence of a human right to the fruit of one's labor while imagining an occasional human right to that of others.[2] Core features of socialism include a push toward pseudo-egalitarianism, abolition of absolute private property rights, rejection of civil liberties, and an assertion that government should manage economies and determine the distribution and use of goods and services.

Karl Marx (1818-1883) and Friedrich Engels (1820-1895), both men of privilege, considered socialism (which had already been intellectually defeated by the time they wrote)[3] the first in a two-stage process leading from capitalism to Communism. They also identified Communism as socialism. In the *Communist Manifesto* Engels wrote,

> [T]he history of the *Manifesto* reflects, to a great extent, the history of the modern working-class movement; at present it is undoubtedly the most widespread, the most international production of all Socialist literature, the common platform acknowledged by millions of workingmen from Siberia to California.[4]

To the extent that Marx and Engels drew a distinction between the two, it was generally to note that Communism is just a type of socialism more open in its embrace of outright revolution as the best way to achieve abolition of private property and implement state ownership (i.e., government monopoly) of the means of production:

---

1. Van Der Linden, Marcel, ed., *The Cambridge History of Socialism* (Cambridge: Cambridge University Press, 2023). 4-7.
2. Although socialists do not tend to present their ideology in this way, I have accurately summed up its essential premise.
3. Ludwig Von Mises, *Marxism Unmasked: From Delusion to Destruction*, (Auburn: Foundation for Economic Education, 2006), 8.
4. Karl Marx and Frederick Engels, *The Communist Manifesto* (New York: International Publishers, 1948), 5.

In France the Communists ally themselves with the Social-Democrats ... In all these movements they bring to the front, as the leading question in each case, the property question ... The Communists disdain to conceal their views and aims. They openly declare that their ends can be attained only by the forcible overthrow of all existing social conditions. Let the ruling classes tremble at a Communist revolution.[5]

Communist Rosa Luxemburg, writing in *Reform or Revolution*, presented socialism as a step that people inside a capitalist system could be persuaded to embrace:

The greatest conquest of the developing proletarian movement has been the discovery of grounds of support for the realization of socialism in the *economic condition* of capitalist society. As a result of this discovery, socialism was changed from an "ideal" dream by humanity for thousands of years to a thing of *historic necessity*.[6]

One of Engels' most popular books, *Socialism: Utopian and Scientific* (original *Socialisme utopique et Socialisme scientifique*), published in 1880, reveals the theory to be a house of cards, passionately but carelessly constructed. The book is filled with praise of then-current fads, as though they were established scientific conclusions.

For example, to support his claim that absolute truth does not exist, Engels wrote that scientists are unable to discern whether a fetus is alive or not. Building on this claim, he presented Hegel's dialectic as more correct than

5. Ibid., 43-44.
6. Rosa Luxemburg, *Reform or Revolution* (New York: Pathfinder Press, 1970), 35.

science.[7] Elsewhere, Engels stated that Darwin "dealt the metaphysical conception of Nature the heaviest blow by his proof that all organic beings, plants, animals, and man himself, are the products of a process of evolution going on through millions of years."[8] No careful scientist, however, refers to Darwin's theory as a proof; it is a theory.

Engels claimed that the materialistic conception of history and revelation of capitalistic production through surplus value—which he referred to as "two great discoveries"—transformed socialism into "a science."[9] That socialism in the 19th Century was in fact a mania carried along by a wave of then-current societal fads and pseudo-scientific theories ought to have been evident to all from the details of Engels' defense of "scientific socialism," but only a fraction of the public seemed to possess the will or ability to make this evaluation.

Ultimately, all socialism, since endorsing theft of labor, is authoritarian. The socialist system wears different masks, behind each of which is always the same face. Put another way, the velvet glove always covers an iron fist. He who resists the chains of the enslavers will soon find himself compelled by the force of the state. Among actual socialist programs in recent U.S. history are student loan "forgiveness," rent control, "affordable housing," Section 8, "Welfare," EBT, WIC, SNAP, progressive income tax, single payer healthcare, tax credits giving "refunds" to those who paid no taxes and any other government scheme that moves wealth from some people to others

---

7. Frederick Engels, *Socialism: Utopian and Scientific, Translated: From The French By Edward Aveling*, Sanage Publishing. Judging from the ongoing debate even today among non-scientific supporters of socialism concerning whether a fetus is alive, we may conclude that the movement has made very little intellectual progress over the last 150 years.

8. Ibid., 55.

9. Ibid., 61.

without the payers' consent.[10] Such programs are doubly unjust when excluding some (typically those who are paying for it) from access to the benefit.

IS IT SOCIALISM?

Socialism contains the word "social," but being "social," or even "cooperative," is not uniquely, or even particularly, descriptive of socialism. In fact, socialism is fairly *anti-social*, since it sanctifies covetousness, greed, and the infringement of the most basic ownership rights of those in the minority. Capitalism, which affirms contracts between people and the right to property acquired through labor, gift, or exchange, is arguably a far more social economic system.

Socialism's advocates sometimes press critics with questions like, "Do you not want roads and schools?"—as though these could not be funded apart from a socialist system. But non-socialist countries regularly fund such important infrastructure and institutions. Here are some common government activities that are not socialism:

- Lawful taxes that treat everyone equally, without respect to wealth, income, or other factors
- Funding basic government activities, including national defense and executive, legislative, and judicial functions through fair taxation
- Funding public infrastructure or services like roads, bridges, and schools, through fair taxation

---

10. EBT=Electronic Benefit Transfer; WIC=Special Supplemental Nutrition Program for Woman, Infants, and Children; SNAP=Supplemental Nutrition Assistance Program (formerly Food Stamps)

- Funding for public health and safety through fair taxation
- The United States' Social Security system, to the extent that it merely pays citizens back in their later years money that they were earlier made to contribute

What about voluntary communal life? Adults joining together, freely consenting to pool their resources, has been called socialism by some and was practiced by the early Christians, as we will see in Chapter 8. However, since its foundation—the affirmation of property—stands opposed to the premise of socialism, we think that such an arrangement is better defined not as socialism, but rather as "cooperative living," or something similar. Such an arrangement can carry a risk for abuse and manipulation, and can leave participants scarred, dependent, and trapped should they ever change their minds, but the voluntary aspect removes the moral cloud of theft from the equation and leaves it a generally benign species of free association. Voluntary communal living or common ownership may merit critique depending upon the details, but it does not generally sink to the level of "socialism."

HOW AND WHY DOES SOCIALISM ADVANCE?

Socialist strategy involves manipulating economic conditions to the harm of the majority, and then leveraging popular greed, envy, or desperation to undermine each individual's legal ownership of his labor and its fruits.[11]

---

11. In this book I employ the convention (standard in English until recently) of writing "he," "him," and "his," when used in a non-specific context, to mean generically "he or she," "him or her," and "his or hers," respectively.

Government seizure of private property and "equitable" redistribution is the result, and in the new environment of abolished or suppressed incentives for enterprise, central government monopoly and control follows.

The main selling point of socialism is the promise of an arrangement in which everyone will have the basic needs of life met, and that removing this worry from their shoulders is a good thing for them and for society. In socialist countries, people don't pay directly for the doctor visits or medical services they use. College is "free." You may even have free or heavily subsidized housing, and you may have a monthly income sent to you from the government. Do all these things sound nice? Sure, if you are not the one paying the bill for all these goods and services.

And even for those generally on the receiving end, it is nice until it isn't—as Charlie Gard's parents (whom you will meet later in this book) discovered. The reality of socialist systems is not always as beautiful as the brochure might suggest. Quality of service is often mediocre and unresponsive, hospitals do not tend to have the best and most current equipment, medical professionals are modestly compensated, there are often long waits for procedures, and there is little opportunity for accountability when things go wrong. Once the system exists, it is often futile to fight it or complain.

One of the preconditions necessary for socialism to take root democratically is for more than half of a population to be willing and motivated to enslave their neighbors. Such a circumstance is difficult to achieve when most people believe they can make ends meet and improve their condition by honest means. It is for this reason that in pre-socialist societies like the United States, advocates for socialism craft policies to impoverish a critical mass of people, moving as many as possible out of relative financial stability and into dependence. This is why, for example, the 2009 U.S. law called Obamacare— as originally passed—was designed to dramatically *raise* costs for healthcare while making it impossible to survive in the health insurance business without government subsidy. Obamacare's unspoken purpose was to greatly enrich a few at the top while draining the savings of middle class Americans and move many more into a state of hopelessness, under which they might vote for politicians promising to redistribute wealth.

Human rights are always an obstacle to socialism. Technically, in my opinion, socialism became illegal in the United States upon passage of the 13th Amendment on December 6, 1865. This amendment abolished involuntary servitude, of which democratic socialism is a type. However, forced wealth redistribution has not yet—to my knowledge—been challenged on these grounds, and so at the time of this writing, mine remains an untested theory. We will discuss this matter in more detail later.

BOILING IT DOWN TO THE ESSENCE

Socialism is a materialist philosophy; thus it treats people as animals, disregards human rights, and often supports murder in the forms of elective abortion, euthanasia, and/or the killing of political opponents. For socialists, justice is ultimately inseparable from the distribution of wealth among people. The root moral assertion of socialists is that material inequality is unjust. In a socialist system, participation is not voluntary and nobody is permitted to opt out. As such, socialism is totalitarian.

By denying property and its disposition while insisting that no one can be satisfied in life so long as someone else (regardless of the reason) enjoys a more pleasant material existence, socialism replaces a healthy fear of God with selfishness and hate of one's neighbor. In place of just trade—e.g., "I'll give you something I have that you want, in exchange for something you have and are willing to give"—it elevates raw power. Socialism says,

"I want what you have, and what I want is all that matters."

Although some socialists profess Christian faith, they often treat scripture carelessly. Pastor Tim Keller,[12] for example, proposed replacing "justice and kindness" in the Bible with "social justice":

> *The Lord loves social justice; the earth is full of his unfailing love.* Psalms 33:5 [Tim Keller translation, as also the next:]

> *This is what the LORD says: "Let not the wise man boast of his wisdom or the strong man boast of his strength or the rich man boast of his riches, but let him who boasts boast about this: that he understands and knows me, that I am the LORD, who exercises kindness and social justice on earth, for in these I delight," declares the LORD.* Jeremiah 9:23-24[13]

Socialist systems include, first, those of Vladimir Lenin, Joseph Stalin, Mao Zedong, Pol Pot, Che Guevara, Kim Il Sung, and Bill Ayers—that is, communism. This type always includes revolution and murder of political opponents, typically labeled "enemies of the State." Communism rarely has the support of a majority; when gaining power, it does so through strategic activity of a well-organized and highly motivated band of activists.

Secondly, there is so-called "democratic socialism," which enables some to seize the property of others by electing wealth-redistributing politicians. Here we find

---

12. Timothy F. Kauffman, "Workers of the Church, Unite!: The Radical Marxist Foundation of Tim Keller's Social Gospel," *Trinity Review* 317-318, (2014): 1-16. See also Megan Basham, *Shepherds For Sale* (New York: Broadside Books, 2024), and Rod Dreher, *Live Not By Lies* (New York: Sentinel, 2020).
13. Tim Keller, *Generous Justice*, Penguin, (New York: Dutton, 2010), 14-15.

Woodrow Wilson, Adolph Hitler, Franklin D. Roosevelt, Howard Zinn, Saul Alinsky, Barack Obama, Eugene V. Debs, Elizabeth Warren, Alexandria Ocasio-Cortez, Kamala Harris, and Bernie Sanders. Communism and "democratic socialism" both reject free markets, deny a right to the fruits of one's own labor, and endorse slavery.

CHAPTER SUMMARY

Socialism, a materialist philosophy rejecting individual ownership of labor and its fruits, is characterized by ultimate government control of property. Socialism asserts that distribution of wealth determines justice. All socialism rejects either God's existence or the Bible's authority, despite sometimes appealing to it. Communism, the silent objective of many socialists, is a late-stage form of socialism. Karl Marx and Frederick Engels, and the Marxist-Leninists, see socialism as the first step in a two-stage process toward total government ownership of the means of production, also known as Communism.

CHAPTER 2

Justice Is Not Mercy, Mercy Is Not Justice

S arah was very happy, and a little nervous, to be driving on her own for the first time. She had recently turned sixteen, and had just passed her driving test in order to get her driver's license. What a good feeling!

It was a beautiful day as Sarah pulled out of her driveway and slowly accelerated. At the intersection, she came to an octagonal red sign bearing the word "STOP." Of course, she knew that this sign meant that she needed to come to a complete stop and then look both ways before proceeding.

But, what if Sarah had somehow come to an understanding that the word "stop" *really* means "go right ahead without pausing"? It would not take long for Sarah to encounter serious trouble, and to become a real danger both to herself and to others.

In any communication there is opportunity for meaning loss, because language is only a symbol representing something else, and because words are "multi-valent," that is, they generally have multiple meanings or shades of meaning. This flexibility makes language incredibly useful, but it also leaves the door open for degradation or distortion of a message as a result of carelessness or malicious manipulation.

But that is not all. Another factor that can lead to misunderstanding is when a recipient intentionally assigns some meaning to a word that was not present in the mind of the one who communicated in the first place. In the example above, if Sarah decided that she just does not like "stop" as it is generally understood, and began to personally insist it really means something different from its plain sense, she would go against the expectation of those who placed the sign. Acting upon her novel definition when approaching stop signs could rightly result in her being held accountable by the governing authorities for any harm she caused.

There is no reason for us to misunderstand the Bible, because in addition to its plain meaning, the Holy Spirit helps us (John 14:26), and God has promised wisdom to all who ask Him (James 1:5). But when people are not interested in hearing from God, it is a different story. Many today treat the Bible as a tool for the advancement of their own purposes. It is nothing new, and it is no wonder, really, since "the Bible says" causes people to stop and listen.

When you receive a message from a friend, you probably want to read it in order to know what he means to say. True, there are times when you misinterpret a message because the words were ambiguous, or because you cannot see the sender's facial expressions or hear his tone of voice. But you rarely make an effort to read the words in a way contrary to what the sender meant.

The Bible is God's letter to you and me. When we come to it, we should see it as such. It is not a multi-tool to be used in pursuit of our preferences or personal agendas. The right approach to the Bible is to work hard to determine what its Author wants us to understand. Reading the Bible to hear what God is saying means that we must not play games with language; it also means that we should watch out for others who may be doing so.

JUSTICE IS NOT MERCY

Justice is a powerful word, and for this reason many people try to claim it. Even those who openly support the most obvious evil sometimes assert that they are the real champions of justice. However, if a word means everything, then it means nothing. So, let's take a moment to clarify what the Bible says about justice.

To begin, the Bible says that *God loves justice*. Psalm 33:5 says, "He loves righteousness and justice; the earth is full of the lovingkindness of the LORD," and Psalm 37:28 tells us, "For the LORD loves justice and does not forsake His godly ones." It is worth noting that the Hebrew word translated "lovingkindness" in Psalm 33:5 is *ḥesed*, which is also sometimes translated "mercy," depending upon context. We will return to that matter later, but for now, just notice that justice and mercy are often mentioned alongside each other in the Bible.

So, God loves justice, but how important is it to Him, really? The Bible answers: "To do righteousness and justice is desired by the LORD more than sacrifice" (Proverbs 21:3). And remember that Jesus had these harsh words for the teachers of the law: "Woe to you, scribes and Pharisees, hypocrites! For you tithe mint and dill and cumin, and have neglected the weightier provisions of the law: justice and mercy and faithfulness; but these are the things you should have done without neglecting the others" (Matthew 23:23; compare with Luke 11:42).

What else does the Bible say about justice? It says that justice *can be practiced*, and that doing so is part of what it takes to live before God:

> "But if a man is righteous and practices justice and righteousness, and does not eat at the mountain shrines

or lift up his eyes to the idols of the house of Israel, or defile his neighbor's wife or approach a woman during her menstrual period—if a man does not oppress anyone, but restores to the debtor his pledge, does not commit robbery, but gives his bread to the hungry and covers the naked with clothing, if he does not lend money on interest or take increase, if he keeps his hand from iniquity and executes true justice between man and man, if he walks in My statutes and My ordinances so as to deal faithfully—he is righteous and will surely live," declares the LORD God. (Ezekiel 18:5-9)

Notice that God's attention in the verses above is upon the *individual*, how he walks day to day, what he does and what he refrains from doing, how he acts toward God and in relationship with other people, and so forth. Although justice is only one of the items on the list of what this man does, the word "justice" returns again near the end: the man acts justly in his own dealings with others, and executes true justice between others—presumably when he is called upon or encounters a situation warranting his involvement.

The presentation of justice as something that is practiced is seen also in Ezekiel 18:19, 33:16, and 45:9. Ezekiel 18:21 and 27, and 33:19 add that the practice of justice is associated with a man turning from his sin and his wickedness. Justice can be *walked in* (Proverbs 8:20)—that is, justice is not something to be done on occasion, but something that should characterize our course of life (see, for example, Ephesians 4:1, 5:8, 1 John 2:6). So, we know how God feels about justice: it is something that people should practice, and walk in, and it is associated with turning away from sin and wickedness. Let's continue.

Biblical justice has a lot to do with relationships between people in terms of contracts and exchanges. Does the God of the universe care about lawsuits between people here on earth? Actually, yes, He does: "To deprive a man of justice in the presence of the Most High, to defraud a man in his lawsuit—of these things the LORD does not approve" (Lamentations 3:35-36). Notice that a man can be deprived of justice "in the presence of the Most High." We know from Psalm 139:7—which says "Where can I go from Your Spirit?"—and elsewhere that God is present everywhere and at all times. So, it is safe to conclude that we owe people justice at all times and are left only to ask, then: What does it mean to deprive a man of justice?

Although justice is not limited to the exchange of goods and services, the Bible most often frames it in economic terms. The basic feature of justice, we find, is *an even standard* that applies consistently for everyone. We will return to this very important aspect in Chapter 13.

Is justice impossible? No, the Bible says that justice in human relationships *can be done*. Jeremiah 22:3 says, "Do justice and righteousness, and deliver the one who has been robbed from the power of his oppressor. Also do not mistreat *or* do violence to the stranger, the orphan, or the widow; and do not shed innocent blood in this place." Notice here that the justice God commands is not limited to our own concerns, but also includes helping others who are being treated unjustly.

Justice can be *spoken*, and it is spoken by the mouth of the righteous (Psalm 37:30). Injustice can be turned from, and justice practiced (Ezekiel 33:14). Justice can be learned and should be sought (Isaiah 1:17). God guards the paths of justice, which can be *discerned* (Proverbs 2:8-9). Humble people will be led and taught by God in justice (Psalm 25:9). We should tremble if we think we know better than God what is just (Job 35:2). God does not pervert justice (Job 34:12). God, rather, brings justice (Job 36:6, Micah 7:9). God will never act unjustly or unrighteously (Job 37:23).

Those who abhor justice twist everything that is

straight (Micah 3:9). Absence of justice is painful (Job 19:7) and displeasing in the sight of the LORD (Isaiah 59:15). We should not be shocked in this fallen world to see justice denied (Ecclesiastes 5:8) and wickedness standing where justice should be (Ecclesiastes 3:16). Some witnesses make a mockery of justice (Proverbs 19:28). The unjust, who do not know the way of peace, have crooked paths with no justice in their tracks (Isaiah 59:8). There are periods when justice is never upheld and the wicked surround the righteous (Habakkuk 1:4), where people's own preferences are considered "justice" (Habakkuk 1:7). The Bible says that when we deny justice, we turn it into wormwood (Amos 5:7) or poison (Amos 6:12).

Even when He seems silent, it is a mistake for anyone to suppose that God does not see our plight (Isaiah 40:27). He will bring justice to light (Zephaniah 3:5). God will judge everyone in the end, and comfort His people (Revelation 20:12, 21:1-4). Zion will be redeemed with justice (Isaiah 1:27). Jesus will proclaim justice to the Gentiles (Matthew 12:18), do justice (Jeremiah 23:5, 33:15), and establish His government with justice and righteousness forever (Isaiah 9:7, 28:17, 42:1-4).

In Jeremiah 22:13, God rebukes kings who build their homes without righteousness and their upper rooms without justice, who use their neighbors' services without pay and who do not give the worker his wages. Laborers are not to be defrauded of their wages (Malachi 3:5). Wages are to be paid promptly (Deuteronomy 24:15). The landowner who pays laborers the agreed-upon wage is the model of God's righteousness (Matthew 20:1-16 [discussed further in Chapter 5]). Failure to pay workers their wages is an injustice that cries out to the Lord (James 5:4).

The oppressed are especially vulnerable to denial of justice (Psalm 146:7), and denial of justice is listed negatively alongside robbery, oppression, wronging the poor and needy, and oppressing the sojourner (Ezekiel 22:29). The needy and the poor are sometimes denied justice (Isaiah 10:2). Plundering the possessions of widows and orphans is the deprivation of justice. Those who deny justice to the alien, orphan, or widow are to be cursed (Deuteronomy 27:19).

Justice is mentioned in the Bible alongside not taking interest and keeping one's hand from iniquity (Ezekiel 18:8). It is mentioned alongside kindness (Hosea 12:6). God commands His people to dispense true justice, and to show kindness toward others (Zechariah 7:9).

Doing justice sometimes takes courage (Micah 3:8). A man who seeks justice and truth can be rare, but can redeem a city (Jeremiah 5:1). Discernment is needed to understand justice (1 Kings 3:11). Justice must be sought and its understanding is not automatic; age does not necessarily bring wisdom, nor understanding of justice (Job 32:9). Evil men do not understand it, but those who seek the LORD do (Proverbs 28:5). Wisdom from God can help in the good administration of justice (1 Kings 3:28). The one who does justice is likened to a person adorned with a robe and turban (Job 29:14). We can remember Solomon's wise administration of justice with discernment from the LORD in the matter of the dispute of two mothers over a baby (I Kings 3:16-27). Those who keep justice are blessed (Psalm 106:3). Doing justice causes things to go well with one (Jeremiah 22:15). Justice is desirable in judgments, and yearned for by the afflicted (Psalm 72:2, 82:3, Isaiah 59:11 and 14, Amos 5:24).

There will be consequences for people who do injustice. The wicked who refuse to act with justice will be dragged away by their own violence (Proverbs 21:7). The exercise of justice is a joy for the righteous, but terror to the workers of iniquity (Proverbs 21:15).

Justice is described as light, and its absence as darkness (Isaiah 59:9). Justice ultimately comes from the LORD, and not from a ruler (Proverbs 29:6). God was not taught justice by anyone (Isaiah 40:14). God is the guardian of justice (Isaiah 49:4). God's justice is a light for the peoples (Isaiah 51:4). God's justice should be preserved because His salvation is imminent (Isaiah 56:1). God will bring justice for His chosen ones who cry to Him day and night (Luke 18:7-8).

Kings are told to do justice, and wisdom is the means by which they decree it (Proverbs 8:20). It can be administered by a good leader (2 Samuel 8:15). Israel's rulers were supposed to know justice (Micah 3:1). Kings can sit on the throne of justice (Proverbs 20:8). God commanded the House of David to administer it morning by morning (Jeremiah 21:12), lest God's wrath go forth like fire and burn with none to extinguish it. It is to be established in the gate (Amos 5:15), alongside hating evil and loving good. God sometimes blesses people with wise and just kings to do justice and righteousness (1 Kings 10:9, 1 Chronicles 18:14, 2 Chronicles 9:8). God tells people to pursue justice only, not for their harm but for their good. The result of doing justice is life in the good land that God is giving to them: "Justice, and only justice, you shall pursue, that you may live and possess the land which the LORD your God is giving you" (Deuteronomy 16:20).

Justice can be perverted by people who go after dishonest gain and who accept bribes (1 Samuel 8:3, Proverbs 17:23). Justice is the means by which a king brings stability to the land, but a man taking bribes overthrows it (Proverbs 29:4). Justice *can be distorted*, something God says not to do: "You shall not distort justice; you shall not be partial, and you shall not take a bribe, for a bribe blinds the eyes of the wise and perverts the words of the righteous" (Deuteronomy 16:19).

Justice is *owed to everyone*, including the alien and the orphan: "You shall not pervert the justice due an alien or an orphan, nor take a widow's garment in pledge. But you shall remember that you were a slave in Egypt, and that the LORD your God redeemed you from there; therefore

I am commanding you to do this thing" (Deuteronomy 24:17-18). Notice here that God immediately reminds the hearers that they themselves were slaves in Egypt—that is, the victims of injustice. It is good to remember that we should not want injustice for others because we do not want it for ourselves. In this verse is a shadow of Jesus' later command, "Treat others the same way you want them to treat you" (Luke 6:31).

Justice is sometimes mentioned alongside *equity* (Psalm 99:4, Proverbs 1:3). Justice, equity and righteousness are *good* (Proverbs 2:9). However, equity must be understood in the Bible's terms. It does not mean wealth redistribution by government, nor does it mean treating people by different standards (see again Leviticus 19:15).

You can see from the foregoing presentation how close to God's heart and how well-defined justice is in the Bible. It is not merely a word to be filled with whatever makes us feel good. It is not something owed only to some people but not to others. Unlike mercy—which we will discuss next—we will *all* get justice for our deeds, both good and bad (Romans 14:10). And importantly, justice is the job of everyone, including governments, at all times.

MERCY IS NOT JUSTICE

Now we turn to mercy. As with justice, we find that the linguistic correspondence between Hebrew and English is not one-to-one. In this case, the Hebrew that most commonly lies behind the word "mercy" in English translations of the Bible is the beautiful word חֶסֶד—*ḥesed*—which can also (depending upon context) be rendered "kindness" or "loving-kindness."[1] Mercy is kindness, and

---

1. Sources consulted for biblical word meanings throughout this book include Robert Young, *Analytical Concordance to the Bible* (Grand Rapids: William B. Eerdmans, 1970) and Ludwig Koehler and Walter

it is not deserved. Rather, it is an expression of love which is an overflowing grace.

Almost always, ḥeṣed in the Bible is something shown, or given, by God. The exceptions are in those verses—such as Micah 6:8, which reads, "He has told you, O man, what is good; and what does the LORD require of you but to do justice, to love kindness, and to walk humbly with your God?"—where God instructs us to do the same. In other words, it seems clear that we are to love ḥeṣed because we are supposed to have a similar heart toward our fellow people as the heart God has for them.

Another word often translated to English as mercy is רחם—raḥam. It means to love, to pity, or to be merciful. Its plural form, raḥamīm, means "bowels" or "mercies," and is found in Genesis 43, Deuteronomy 13, Nehemiah 1, and Isaiah 47. A third Hebrew word translated as mercy is חנן—ḥanan—means "to be gracious or inclined to." The general Greek word translated "mercy," ελεος—eleos—meaning kindness or beneficence, appears in the New Testament and the Septuagint.

Mercy is *good*, but it is not justice; it is forgiveness of a debt. It is kindness when kindness is not obligated or owed. And importantly, mercy is generally the duty of individuals, not government or corporate bodies. Throughout the Bible, mercy is often mentioned alongside justice, usually after justice (i.e., "justice and mercy," rather than "mercy and justice"). Indeed, in some situations, mercy only makes sense in the context of, or in contrast to, justice. Mercy is not the opposite of justice, or even the denial of justice, but gentle forbearance in the application of justice. And, ḥeṣed can also mean out-of-the-blue, unexpected, and even overwhelming kindness that has nothing, really, to do with justice. For example, in

---

Baumgartner, *The Hebrew and Aramaic Lexicon of the Old Testament* (Leiden: Brill, 2001).

Genesis 39:21, we find that the LORD extended *ḥesed* to Joseph while he was (wrongly) held in jail.

It is critical not to miss how special and powerful the word *ḥesed* is, and above all how *personal* it is. In contrast to justice, lovingkindness—or mercy (*ḥesed*)—is not a job for government, particularly where government is not the offended party. A king might possibly show lovingkindness to a peer, to an enemy, or to a subject. But how could a bureaucrat, or an agency, or a committee, or a panel ever embody such a thing as *ḥesed*?

The answer, I believe, is that it cannot. And here we see the critical distinction between justice and mercy: justice can be administered by government, because it is an administrative task that relies simply upon discovering the facts in a case and then applying the law with impartiality. That is a tremendously different thing from showing lovingkindness or mercy. Justice is matter-of-fact, while mercy is *always* personal. This fact is a core reason that it is entirely inappropriate and misguided to lump justice and mercy together as though they are somehow different words for the very same thing.

Who can extend mercy? This question brings us to the very heart of the matter. In fact, mercy can only be shown by the one who has been wronged, or by a representative who has been given authority to act on behalf of the one who was wronged.

EXAMPLES OF INJUSTICE AND UNKINDNESS

Would a tax credit given exclusively to people below a certain level of income or wealth be unjust? How about a higher bar for college admissions for a person of one race over another? Or a decision by a police chief or judge to exempt certain people (such as noncitizens, or people of certain racial or ethnic backgrounds) from prosecution for crimes? Would it be unjust to make descendants of

21

19th century abolitionists (or, for that matter, immigrants who were not even present for our great national fight over slavery) pay reparations to descendants of 19th century slaves because of the actions of 19th century American slaveholders? What about withholding painting lessons from a young and talented Picasso in order to level the playing field in art, since many others do not have such talent—would that be unjust?

Some form of each of these examples has been presented by advocates of "social justice" as if it were just. My belief is that all of them are *unjust*. Actual justice is not limited to one person or group or sphere, and the moment it is so limited—using words such as "social," or "economic," or "environmental," or "reproductive"—it is transformed to injustice. God is the Judge. I present them for your consideration and propose that we can correctly assess such matters by careful attention.

HOW ARE JUSTICE AND MERCY RELATED?

Justice and mercy are both good things in God's eyes, but they are *different things*, and anyone who says they are not is a false teacher who ought to be rebuked and excluded from a position of Christian authority.[2] Lovingkindness (*hesed*) is appropriate at all times (Proverbs 3:3), but *mercy* as we understand it in English is not appropriate in every situation. We know this to be true, because if mercy *were* to be required in every circumstance

---

2. "Be on guard for yourselves and for all the flock, among which the Holy Spirit has made you overseers, to shepherd the church of God which He purchased with His own blood. I know that after my departure savage wolves will come in among you, not sparing the flock; and from among your own selves men will arise, speaking perverse things, to draw away the disciples after them. Therefore be on the alert, remembering that night and day for a period of three years I did not cease to admonish each one with tears" (Acts 20:28-31).

—and if it were applied in every circumstance, then *there would be no justice*. Imagine:

> "Great job, team. After years of investigation, millions of taxpayer dollars, and expert police work in partnership with the FBI, we finally captured and prosecuted the notorious Blue Mountain serial killer and rapist. The families of his 47 victims will never see their loved ones again, but they can at least rest in the knowledge that the killer is facing justice, will spend the rest of his life in prison, and will never harm another innocent victim—"
>
> *"Excuse me!"*
>
> "Who are you?"
>
> *"Ned Schnoodle, Federal Department of Mercy (FDM), formerly Department of Social Justice. Now that the accused has been found guilty and sentenced, the next step, according to guidelines issued last month and the decision of the three member FDM panel (who judge the killer 'downtrodden') is to set him free. You have no right to hold him; as our doctrine clearly states, 'Justice equals mercy; Mercy is a human right for the downtrodden.' We'll take it from here, folks..."*
>
> "Wait a minute! These families are owed justice."
>
> *"Ma'am, as the Bible says, 'Mercy triumphs over judgment' (James 2:13), and 'Judge not, lest you be judged' (Matthew 7:1). Have a nice day!"*

Ned Schnoodle is engaged in theological malpractice. There is a place for mercy, but Ned's application of scripture is wrong. Mercy is not the same thing as justice. To the contrary, it is the unmerited nature of mercy that makes it so special and good. Justice is *owed* to people. Everyone has a right to it. When justice is not done, people are harmed. Mercy (that is, lovingkindness)—even though you and I have an individual duty to *love* it (Micah 6:8)—is by its very definition not owed to *anyone*.

WE SHOULD AVOID FAKE JUSTICE AND FALSE MERCY

Many of our left-leaning friends wrongly aim for everything to be run by the government. They say they want justice, but then treat justice as though it is only owed to some people—which is contrary to what the Bible says—and they say they want mercy, but fail to grasp that government typically *can't* give mercy without doing injustice.

So-called "social justice" includes many causes, some worthy but many not. One common error of "social justice" advocates is that of making a genuine injustice whose victims are long dead into the pretext for a hustle in which people who played no part in the wrong are made to pay restitution to people other than the actual victims.

It should now be clear that justice and mercy, while both important, are very different things. So, like Sarah reading the stop sign as though it really meant "go right ahead," it would be a serious error to treat justice and mercy as though they were the same thing. Those who twist the Bible to serve a socialist agenda pretend that justice and mercy are interchangeable terms. But, I believe scripture is clear that, while the words do belong together, it is critical to keep their meanings distinct—and failing to do so can cause us to perpetrate *injustice* and to be *unmerciful*.

CHAPTER SUMMARY

Justice, or equal treatment and honest dealing under the law, is owed to everyone. God loves justice and commands it. God also loves mercy and He tells us to love it too. In contrast to justice, mercy is undeserved kindness, a voluntary expression of love shown by someone to another who wronged him, or a personal and self sacrificial extension of help. Mercy, by definition, is never owed. If someone wronged you, the choice to show or withhold mercy is entirely yours. Forced kindness is not kindness; compelled love is not love. This is why we hear of mercy being sought, even *begged for*, but never demanded—unless by someone who misunderstands the word.

To get around the voluntary nature of mercy, which does not serve socialist objectives, those who wish to assert that receiving mercy is a right rather than a personal gift often conflate mercy and justice, insisting that mercy is *owed* and is a job for government. In so doing, they invariably do *injustice*.

CHAPTER 3

Justice Prefers Neither Poor Nor Rich

You shall do no injustice in judgment; you shall not be partial to the poor nor defer to the great, but you are to judge your neighbor fairly. (Leviticus 19:15)

D id you know that it is a *sin* to extend a preferential option to the poor in judgment, and that the person who does so is every bit as guilty of injustice as the one who shows partiality to a rich person? Exodus 23:3 says it too. That's right, according to the Bible, justice demands that there be no favoritism in judgment. Everyone, whether rich or poor, is owed the same standard before the law.

But what, you may be thinking, are we to make of Jesus' care for the poor, the fact that He sought out their company and placed an emphasis upon them in His teaching? It is true that God cares for the poor, and we will address that fact directly in the next chapter, but before doing so, we need to give our attention to the critical feature of justice: It shows no partiality to anyone. In other words, the poor do not get the benefit of the doubt or a "get out of jail free" pass in the courts of law.

Poor people are owed fairness and impartiality in judgment—an even standard. They must not be dismissed or written off or treated as though they are less deserving of justice because of their humble means or lack of power and influence. That is God's commandment. Poor people have a *right* to justice, but this right makes them *equal* in standing to everyone else, *not* higher:

> Hear the cases between your fellow countrymen, and judge righteously between a man and his fellow countryman, or the alien who is with him. You shall not show partiality in judgment; you shall hear the small and the great alike. (Deuteronomy 1:16-17)

UNDERSTANDING WEALTH AND POVERTY

Material wealth is the tangible residue of labor—either our own or that of the person from whom we received it by gift or exchange or inheritance. Wealth is the potential to acquire useful goods or services.[1] Because our life and strength are a gift from God, so also any wealth we have is a gift from Him, one that is entrusted to us for a while.

Wealth levels change over the course of any person's lifetime, and possessions are fleeting. Wealth grows or diminishes based partly on our hard work combined with diligent and wise cultivation and care of what we have over time, and also partly upon circumstances beyond our control. It is possible to be very poor, and then rich, and then poor again. Sometimes people move in and out of socio-economic categories multiple times. Such mobility

---

1. As the economist Adam Smith observed, "Every man is rich or poor according to the degree in which he can afford to enjoy the necessaries, conveniences, and amusements of human life." Adam Smith, *An Inquiry into the Nature and Causes of the Wealth of Nations*, Norwalk: Easton Press (1991), 27-8.

throughout life is invisible on most bar graphs that show the distribution of wealth or earnings.

Although we often act otherwise, possessions are not the defining factor or substance in a person's life or happiness. As Jesus said, "Beware, and be on your guard against every form of greed; for not even when one has an abundance does his life consist of his possessions" (Luke 12:15).

Moreover, there is a special depth of character and blessing that can come with being poor. This observation is not an excuse for keeping people poor, but merely an acknowledgment that hardship can help us to grow as human beings in ways that we might never do if we always have it easy. This truth was referenced by James: "Consider it all joy, my brethren, when you encounter various trials, knowing that the testing of your faith produces endurance. And let endurance have its perfect result, so that you may be perfect and complete, lacking in nothing" (James 1:2-4). James reminds us that difficulties are a gift from God. Athletes demonstrate the same principle in training: resistance develops strength.

Although it is not entirely clear that He was speaking specifically about poverty in terms of possessions, I expect that our refinement through hardship at God's direction and by His grace is part of what Jesus meant when he taught, "Blessed are the poor in spirit, for theirs is the kingdom of heaven. Blessed are those who mourn, for they shall be comforted" (Matthew 5:3-4). If we presume that a life of ease is the way to fulfillment, we will miss some of life's great joys. Many people who have wealth without a right spiritual perspective learn this lesson the hard way as their emptiness grows in the midst of what the outside world views as a perfect situation.

THE POWER OF TRUTH

Socialism is not merely a political construct. It is ultimately a spiritual attack, a lie that can steal a man's life on earth and keep him away from eternal life with God in heaven. The lie is this: Your life consists in your material possessions, and you cannot be happy, you cannot be whole, you cannot be satisfied in life, until you have "social justice." Until then, you must remain angry, resentful, and hateful toward those who have more.

The tragedy of bitterness and envy is that they do not only—nor even mainly—harm the person who is hated and envied. More than anything, they steal the joy of the person who hates.

There is a time for hate (Ecclesiastes 3:8). But the only biblical directions we have indicating the appropriate object of hate is nonhuman: "Let love be without hypocrisy. Abhor what is evil; cling to what is good. Be devoted to one another in brotherly love" (Romans 12:9-10), "Hate evil, you who love the LORD" (Psalm 97:10), "From your precepts I get understanding; therefore I hate every false way" (Psalm 119:104; similar to verses 128 and 163), "A righteous man hates falsehood" (Proverbs 13:5), and "Hate evil, love good, and establish justice in the gate!" (Amos 5:15). One example of commendable hate in action is found in Exodus 18:21, where Jethro advises Moses to select leaders who hate dishonest gain.

The Bible in many places reports people hating other people, but, although David records some autobiographical exclamations in a couple places, ("Do I not hate those who hate You, O LORD? And do I not loathe those who rise up against You? I hate them with the utmost hatred; they have become my enemies" [Psalm 139:21-22]), and although there are a couple types of people the Bible says God hates ("a false witness who utters lies" and "one who spreads strife among brothers" [Proverbs 6:19]), the Bible does not in any place tell you or me to hate anyone in the common sense of that word. Rather, it says that while we may reprove a neighbor, we may not hate him in our heart (Leviticus 19:17), and indeed, we are supposed to love our enemies, and do good to those who hate us (Luke 6:27). The one who hates his brother is said to be in the darkness, walking in the darkness, and does not know where he is going because the darkness has blinded his eyes (1 John 2:9 and 11), "Everyone who hates his brother is a murderer" (1 John 3:15), and "If someone says, 'I love God,' and hates his brother, he is a liar" (1 John 4:20).

Jesus does require His followers to "hate" their own father and mother and wife and children and brothers and sisters (Luke 14:26), but since we know from other places that His command is to love others (e.g., the second greatest commandment is to "love your neighbor as yourself," and the fifth commandment says to "Honor your father and your mother"), I believe it is correct to understand it to mean that His followers' love for Him and willingness to follow Him wherever He leads must be so great that their love for these others would appear as hate by comparison.

One awful effect of socialism is that it invites people to postpone joy that is available to them *right now*, and *regardless of circumstance*, until a future date that may never arrive. It also invites people to hate their neighbor, the "oppressor," the one with marginally more property (even if honestly gained and justly held), or the one who is perceived to have some other advantage in life. And we have already seen that hate hurts the hater most of all.

There is a better way. Your sins can be forgiven. No matter what you have done, thought, or said, you can be washed clean and justified before God—not because of your goodness ("By the works of the Law no flesh will be justified in His sight" [Romans 3:20]), but because of what Jesus did for you.

Jesus said, "For God so loved the world, that He gave His only begotten Son, that whoever believes in Him shall not perish, but have eternal life" (John 3:16). And, in John 10:10, He said, "The thief comes only to steal and kill and destroy; I came that they may have life, and have it abundantly." Jesus came to give us both *eternal* life and *abundant* life. I believe that, among other things, this promised abundant life includes the items listed in Galatians 5:22-23: love, joy, peace, patience, kindness, goodness, faithfulness, gentleness, and self-control.

Romans 3:23 reports our universal problem: "all have sinned and fall short of the glory of God," and Romans 6:23 states that "the wages of sin is death." Wages are what is earned. If you have sinned, according to the Bible, you've earned death. "But," Romans 5:8-9 says, "God demonstrates His own love toward us, in that while we were yet sinners, Christ died for us. Much more then, having now been justified by His blood, we shall be saved from the wrath of God through Him." And, 1 Corinthians 15:3-4 tells us, "that Christ died for our sins, according to the Scriptures, and that He was buried, and that He was raised on the third day according to the Scriptures." And Jesus stated plainly, "I am the way, and the truth, and the life; no one comes to the Father but through Me" (John 14:6). How is this gift claimed? "But as many as received Him, to them He gave the right to become children of God, even to those who believe in His name" (John 1:12), and, "if the Son makes you free, you will be free indeed" (John 8:36).

Have you trusted Jesus? If you want what is promised above, you can follow Him now and receive joy that is not contingent upon your material circumstances. Pray something like this: "Jesus, I need You. Thank You for loving me and for dying on the cross for my sins. I am a sinner, I recognize my sin, and I am sorry. I turn from my sin to follow You. I trust You alone to cover my sin and make me a child of God."

CHAPTER SUMMARY

Justice, by definition, is an even standard. Giving preference in matters of law to one person over another, whether in the name of poverty, or disadvantage in life, or diversity, equity, and inclusion, is a *sin* according to the Bible. As Leviticus 19:15 says, "You shall do no injustice in judgment; you shall not be partial to the poor nor defer to the great, but you are to judge your neighbor fairly." No one who loves justice should have anything to do with such preferential treatment for anyone.

CHAPTER 4

God Cares for the Poor, and So Should We

Are not two sparrows sold for a cent? And yet not one of them will fall to the ground apart from your Father. But the very hairs of your head are numbered. So do not fear; you are more valuable than many sparrows. (Matthew 10:29-31)

The very idea that God—who made and governs a trillion trillion stars and planets, the far reaches of the universe, every animal and plant, every ocean and mountain—would have a personal concern for any one of us should be stunning. We are like ants! And we have no idea of the worlds and wonders He made that exist a billion light years away from our own.

And yet, we are told by Jesus that God, in His care for us, numbers even the hairs of our head (Matthew 10:30; Luke 12:7). Why? And what can it mean?

GOD SEES AND LOOKS AFTER THE POOR

God's care is for everyone, including the apparently small

and insignificant. In Psalm 23, David reflects upon the fact that God watches over his way:

> The LORD is my shepherd, I shall not want. He makes me lie down in green pastures; He leads me beside quiet waters. He restores my soul; He guides me in the paths of righteousness for His name's sake.
>
> Even though I walk through the valley of the shadow of death, I fear no evil, for You are with me; Your rod and Your staff, they comfort me. You prepare a table before me in the presence of my enemies; You have anointed my head with oil; my cup overflows. Surely goodness and lovingkindness will follow me all the days of my life, and I will dwell in the house of the LORD forever.

The Hebrew for *my shepherd*, רעי—*ro'i*—literally means "my watcher." It is personal, just as being a shepherd is personal. Consider that "The LORD," Maker of the universe, is "*my*" shepherd.

David was the youngest and smallest in his family, yet God lifted him up. Was he (who was, after all, chosen by God) just a special case? Yes, in terms of being chosen, but not in terms of God's knowledge and care. The Bible reminds us many times of His great love: the LORD hears the needy and does not despise His own who are prisoners (Psalm 69:33).[1] He will maintain the cause of the afflicted and justice for the poor (Psalm 140:12), have compassion on the poor and needy and save their lives

---

1. The biblical words relating to poverty and neediness include אביון—*ebyon*—"needy, miserable, poor," דל—*dal*—"scanty, poor, sparse, helpless," ענה—*'aneh*—"humble, poor, humiliated, oppressed," עני—*'ani*—"wretched, oppressed," מוך—*mukh*—"to be or become low or impoverished," רוש—*rush*—"to be poor socially or economically," ירש—*yarash*—"to become impoverished," πτωχος—*ptōchos*—"trembling, poor," πτωχευω *ptōcheuō* "to be or become poor," and πενιχρος *penichros* "very poor."

(Psalm 72:13). He stands at the right hand of the needy, to save him (Psalm 109:31), has delivered the soul of the needy one from the hand of evildoers (Jeremiah 20:13), from the one who is too strong for him (Psalm 35:10), and gives him justice (Job 36:6, 15). The LORD sets the needy securely on high away from affliction (Psalm 107:41), saves the poor from the hand of the mighty so the helpless has hope and unrighteousness must shut its mouth (Job 5:15-16), raises them from the dust and lifts the needy from the ash heap to make them sit with nobles (1 Samuel 2:8, Psalm 113:7), and is their refuge (Psalm 14:6). The Bible assures us that the needy will not always be forgotten (Psalm 9:18); God will answer (Isaiah 41:17), and will deliver when he cries for help (Psalm 72:12). Isaiah said that God has "been a defense for the helpless, a defense for the needy in his distress" (Isaiah 25:4).

Everyone will give an answer to God for what they have done (2 Corinthians 5:10). And while we yearn for justice in this life, we may also be assured that He will make *everything* right in the end: "But with righteousness He will judge the poor, and decide with fairness for the afflicted of the earth; and He will strike the earth with the rod of His mouth, and with the breath of His lips He will slay the wicked" (Isaiah 11:4; cf. Revelation 7:17, 21:4).

WE SHOULD SEE PEOPLE WITH GOD'S EYES

In the years soon after Jesus' resurrection, James gave instructions to the believers at Jerusalem, to counter the human inclination to favor those whom one might perceives as being more likely to benefit him personally:

> My brethren, do not hold your faith in our glorious Lord Jesus Christ with an attitude of personal favoritism. For if a man comes into your assembly with a gold ring and dressed in fine clothes, and there also comes in a poor man in dirty clothes, and you pay spe-

cial attention to the one who is wearing the fine clothes, and say, "You sit here in a good place," and you say to the poor man, "You stand over there, or sit down by my footstool," have you not made distinctions among yourselves, and become judges with evil motives? Listen, my beloved brethren: did not God choose the poor of this world to be rich in faith and heirs of the kingdom which He promised to those who love Him? But you have dishonored the poor man. Is it not the rich who oppress you and personally drag you into court? Do they not blaspheme the fair name by which you have been called?

If, however, you are fulfilling the royal law according to the Scripture, "YOU SHALL LOVE YOUR NEIGHBOR AS YOURSELF," you are doing well. But if you show partiality, you are committing sin and are convicted by the law as transgressors. (James 2:1-9)

And the first century Jerusalem church showed concern for the poor, a concern shared by Paul: "They only asked us to remember the poor—the very thing I also was eager to do" (Galatians 2:10).

While the above instructions were given to believers, God's moral law is universal. Accordingly, His rebuke is leveled against Israel and against the nations at various times. God said He found the lifeblood of the innocent poor on Israel's garments even though they were not breaking and entering (Jeremiah 2:34). Nathan called King David to account for oppressing the poor Uriah, stealing his only wife (2 Samuel 12:1-9). God blamed those who rob the needy of justice and the poor of their rights (Isaiah 10:2), the city of Sodom for—among other things—not helping the poor and needy (Ezekiel 16:49), and Israel in Ezekiel's time for—among other things— wronging the poor and needy (Ezekiel 22:29). He faulted them for distressing the righteous, accepting bribes, and turning aside the poor in the gate (Amos 5:12).

In the following passage, the prophet Amos reports God's promise that the *land will quake* because of Israel's mistreatment of the poor of his time. "Income disparity," of course, is not presented as a moral problem here or anywhere else in the Bible; the problem in this case was *cheating* with dishonest scales:

> Hear this, you who trample the needy, to do away with the humble of the land, saying, "When will the new moon be over, so that we may sell grain, and the sabbath, that we may open the wheat market, to make the bushel smaller and the shekel bigger, and to cheat with dishonest scales, so as to buy the helpless for money, and the needy for a pair of sandals, and that we may sell the refuse of the wheat?" The LORD has sworn by the pride of Jacob, "Indeed, I will never forget any of their deeds. Because of this will not the land quake and everyone who dwells in it mourn?" (Amos 8:4-8; see also 2:6).

Poverty not only carries with it uncertainty, it impacts human relationships. The Bible says that the poor man is hated even by his neighbor, while the rich are loved by many (Proverbs 14:20), and that the poor man is hated by his brothers and abandoned by his friends (Proverbs 19:7). In Ecclesiastes 5:8, Solomon wrote that the poor and weak often have scant ability to push back against injustice, as well as the structure of power that can lead people who might otherwise do the right thing to let it continue: "If you see oppression of the poor and denial of justice and righteousness in the province, do not be shocked at the sight; for one official watches over another official, and there are higher officials over them." The writer of Ecclesiastes also depicted the anguish of those denied justice:

Then I looked again at all the acts of oppression which were being done under the sun. And behold I saw the tears of the oppressed and that they had no one to comfort them; and on the side of their oppressors was power, but they had no one to comfort them (Ecclesiastes 4:1).

Why does God allow great suffering in the first place? In the oldest book in the Bible, Job asks why God does not stop various evildoers, among them those who "push the needy aside from the road," while "the poor of the land are made to hide themselves altogether" (Job 24:4). The wicked man is said by one of Job's friends to have oppressed and forsaken the poor (Job 20:19). These are not new questions. Part of the answer is that God works even great tragedy to a good end, in ways we may not be able to see (Romans 8:28). But judgment is coming for those who oppress the poor and crush the needy (e.g., Amos 4:1-3).

ONE WHO HELPS THE POOR DOES A GOOD THING

Jeremiah 22:16 states that helping the cause of the poor is part of what it means to know God. In the midst of his suffering, Job protested that he had *not* neglected to show kindness to the poor:

If I have kept the poor from their desire, or have caused the eyes of the widow to fail, or have eaten my morsel alone, and the orphan has not shared it (but from my youth he grew up with me as a father, and from infancy I guided her), if I have seen anyone perish for lack of clothing, or that the needy had no covering, if his loins have not thanked me, and if he has not been warmed with the fleece of my sheep, if I have lifted up my hand against the orphan, because I saw I had support in the gate, let my shoulder fall from the socket, and my arm be broken off at the elbow. (Job 31:16-22, cf. 29:12,16)

How should we act toward poor people? Proverbs tells us not to rob them or crush them (22:22) and says that he who is gracious to them is happy (14:21), that if we shut our ear to their cry, we will also cry and not be answered (21:13), and that the one who oppresses them to make more for himself will only come to poverty (22:16). Conversely, Psalm 41:1 promises that he who considers the helpless will be blessed, and the LORD will deliver him in a day of trouble.

Proverbs says that he who is gracious to the poor is happy (14:21); that he who oppresses (14:31) or mocks (17:5) them taunts their Maker, while he who is gracious to them honors Him; that we lend to God, who will repay us, by being gracious to a poor man (19:17); that those who include among their acts of generosity feeding the poor will be blessed (22:9, cf. Psalm 112:1,9); and that the one who gives to them will never want (28:27). The righteous is concerned for the rights of the poor (29:7), and the throne of a king who judges them with truth will be established forever (29:14). And, Psalm 82:3-4 tells us to vindicate the weak and fatherless, do justice to the afflicted and destitute, rescue the weak and needy, and deliver them out of the hand of the wicked.

We have already seen God's concern for the poor recorded in the time of Job. But God's instructions to the people of Israel through Moses are specific. For example,

> If there is a poor man with you, one of your brothers, in any of your towns in your land which the LORD your God is giving you, you shall not harden your heart, nor close your hand from your poor brother; but you shall freely open your hand to him, and shall generously lend him sufficient for his need in whatever he lacks. (Deuteronomy 15:7-8)

Notice in this passage that while God commanded generosity and an open hand, He did *not* command the leveling of wealth. The concern is only that the brother has sufficient for his *need*. Also, it is only commanded to help the poor brother by *lending*; although it was to be without interest if the person was a fellow Israelite (Exodus 22:25, Leviticus 25:35-36, Deuteronomy 23:19-20), it was not inappropriate to expect to be repaid in due course. Furthermore, we learn that *not* helping in such a circumstance would be sin (Deuteronomy 15:9).

THE MORAL LAW APPLIES TO EVERYONE

The frequent mention of justice for the poor in the Bible has caused some to suppose that this means the poor are the only people owed justice, on the one hand, and that the poor can do no wrong, on the other. Neither is true. Poor people are vulnerable, indeed, but the moral law applies to *everyone*, and that includes poor people. For example, Proverbs 28:3 reminds us that poor people can be oppressors too (see also Matthew 18:28-30), and Proverbs 30:8-9 makes clear that the command not to steal applies to a poor person just as much as to anyone else.

POOR AND RICH ARE EQUAL BEFORE GOD

Material wealth impresses many people. God, however, sees the heart (1 Samuel 16:7). In Proverbs, we read that a poor man who walks in his integrity is better than a fool (19:1), that what is desirable in a man is his kindness, and that poverty is preferable to dishonesty (19:22, cf. 28:6). We find a similar observation in Ecclesiastes 4:13: "A poor yet wise lad is better than an old and foolish king who no longer knows how to receive instruction." Time and chance overtake everyone (Ecclesiastes 9:11). God does not regard the rich above the poor; all are the work of His hands (Job 34:19). The poor has the same Maker as the rich (Proverbs 22:22).

God has no need. Rather, He knows that voluntary generosity is *good for us*, both for the receiver and the one who gives. Generosity is one way of cultivating our trust in God, our love for Him, and a healthy love for our neighbor. And everyone should practice giving. The poor widow put two small copper coins in the treasury after the rich had brought their more lavish offerings, and Jesus (seeing this) said, "Truly I say to you, this poor widow put in more than all of them; for they all out of their surplus put into the offering; but she out of her poverty put in all that she had to live on" (Luke 21:3-4, cf. Mark 12:43-44). Jesus saw the truth, and was pleased with the faith of that widow.

OUR INDIVIDUAL OBLIGATION TO THE POOR

What does care for the poor that pleases God look like in practice? Does it mean the forced leveling of wealth? Punishing or hating the rich? Government programs? Placing roadblocks and burdensome regulations in the way of those who are more well-off? The details are important. One of the most famous (and most abused, in my observation) passages in the Bible is Micah 6:8: "He has told you, O man, what is good; and what does the LORD require of you but to do justice, to love kindness, and to walk humbly with your God?"

The first thing to remember about this verse, as we saw in Chapter 2, is that justice and kindness (also sometimes translated "mercy") are two different things. The second is that justice is owed to everyone and must be *done*. The third is that God sees kindness (mercy) as good, and requires us to love it. The fourth is that He expects us to walk humbly with Him.

When God gave Daniel the meaning of King Nebuchadnezzar's dream, it was one of judgment against the king. But Daniel also offered the king a suggestion: "Break away now from your sins by doing righteousness and from your iniquities by showing mercy to the poor" (Daniel 4:27). Although Nebuchadnezzar was not a Hebrew, all people are morally accountable to their Creator. Notice that Daniel called the king to turn from his sins and show mercy to the poor. This advice is quite similar to the commands of Micah 6:8, and the guidance is a general statement of what is right; it applies to you and me as well.

Many ceremonial commands are detailed in Exodus, Numbers, and Deuteronomy. Later, fasting was associated with mourning, repentance, or seeking God's help or guidance. Although it is right do what God said, obedience should not make us self-righteous; the law shows us our need (Galatians 3:24). And we must not forget to help others while being so busy trying to please God! Isaiah rebuked Israel, saying the fast God chooses is "to loosen the bonds of wickedness, to undo the bands of the yoke, and to let the oppressed go free and break every yoke," and "to divide your bread with the hungry and bring the homeless poor into the house; when you see the naked, to cover him" (Isaiah 58:6-7). Do you want to do what is right? Among your activities should be showing concern for your needy neighbor whom God loves (John 21:15-17, 1 John 3:17).

Generosity that reflects God's lovingkindness toward us is one key to how we ought to act toward those who are in perilous need around us.

BLESSED ARE THE POOR IN SPIRIT

What if *you* are poor? There is an old hymn: "When upon life's billows you are tempest tossed / When you are discouraged, thinking all is lost / Count your many blessings, name them one by one / And it will surprise you what the

Lord has done."[2] Can poverty and suffering be a gift? As we saw earlier, James said we should be joyful when facing trials, because we know that God uses them to develop perseverance, to make us mature and complete (James 1:2-4). No matter how hard our lives, we can always be thankful.

While Jesus' teaching on the beatitudes in the Sermon on the Mount (Matthew 5:1-12, Luke 6:20-26) did not focus solely upon people's material circumstances, I believe that the message is similar to what James wrote. Although our physical well-being is important, our joy ought to be based upon something much deeper than material circumstances, a quiet trust in God's care for us and in His faithfulness to make all things right in the end.

JESUS DID NOT REFER TO POVERTY AS EVIL

The gospel writers report Jesus becoming indignant on several occasions—when encountering a man with a debilitating health condition (Mark 1:41); upon death of a friend He loved (John 11:33); with the desecration of God's temple by commercial activity (John 2:14-16, Matthew 21:12-13, Mark 11:15-17); at His disciples' effort to keep the children away from Him (Mark 10:14); and at those who prioritized ritualistic observance over doing good and saving a life (Mark 3:5). However, we have no record of Jesus ever pronouncing poverty or inequality of wealth to be evil.

To the contrary, Jesus accepted poverty as part of life. He did not decry the economic condition of the poor; He came to preach the gospel to them (Matthew 11:5, Luke 4:18, 7:22). The word "gospel" means "good news." What was the good news for the poor? Was it news of material equity, of wealth redistribution, of massacring or dispossessing or exiling of the wealthy? Absolutely not.

2. Johnson Oatman, Jr., 1897.

Jesus said, "You will always have the poor with you" (Matthew 26:11, Mark 14:7, John 12:8). By this statement, I do not believe Jesus canceled our obligation to show kindness to the poor; He simply recognized that the opportunity to do so would always exist (Deuteronomy 15:11). The good news for the poor had nothing to do with their bank accounts and everything to do with the fact that their sins could be forgiven, that—regardless of temporary material circumstance—they could take complete joy in the gift of God, the perfect sacrifice for remission of sins that Jesus was about to make of Himself, in the fullest and deepest expression of lovingkindness this world ever saw.

But why the poor, specifically? Why was the good news not brought to everyone? Actually, it was. On the one hand, preaching the gospel to the poor was a specific part of the prophecy of Messiah in Isaiah 61:1. And Jesus was, indeed, born in low condition and preached the gospel to those in humble circumstances. But the poor—the word in Isaiah means "afflicted" or "humble"—is not limited to material condition, and is (I believe) related to Jesus' statement, "Blessed are the poor in spirit, for theirs is the kingdom of heaven" (Matthew 5:3). The gift that He extends is for all who are afflicted—that's every one of us—and who are humble in recognition of our need.

God's kindness should be reflected in our lives, and should be genuine. One way to ensure your acts of kindness are not really self-serving is to do them in secret (Matthew 6:3, 6:6, 6:18) or to do them to those who have no way of repaying you. Jesus said that when we give dinners or receptions, we should invite the poor and those with physical handicaps who are unable to repay us (Luke 14:13, 21). Have you ever done that? It is something to consider.

What is our ultimate obligation to the poor? It is to do justice—for example, by not cheating them and by ensuring that they are judged with an even standard in the courts—and to love kindness:

> Zaccheus stopped and said to the Lord, "Behold, Lord, half of my possessions I will give to the poor, and if I have defrauded anyone of anything, I will give back four times as much." And Jesus said to him, "Today salvation has come to this house, because he, too, is a son of Abraham" (Luke 19:8-9).

We will look more deeply at what God says about caring for needy neighbors in Chapter 10-12.

CHAPTER SUMMARY

There are many good reasons that we should help our neighbor who is in serious need. We should do it because we would like the same done to us. We should do it because loving our neighbor is a good thing. We should do it because God tells us to do it. We should do it because caring for others is good for our own soul. And, we should do it in humble recognition that we ourselves have benefitted from God's grace and blessings, and caring for others is a natural and fitting expression of gratitude for what He did for us—one that also pleases God.

CHAPTER 5

"Have You Considered My Servant Job?"

For a hundred years, Communist agitators have pushed for "the rich" to pay their "fair share"—by which they mean far more than others pay. To them, "the rich" are villains, enemies of the people. In the Communist worldview, equality of outcome is justice.

> There was a man in the land of Uz whose name was Job; and that man was blameless, upright, fearing God and turning away from evil ... His possessions also were 7,000 sheep, 3,000 camels, 500 yoke of oxen, 500 female donkeys, and very many servants; and that man was the greatest of all the men of the east ... The LORD said to Satan, "Have you considered My servant Job? For there is no one like him on the earth, a blameless and upright man, fearing God and turning away from evil." (Job 1:1, 3, 8)

He was the wealthiest man of the east ... and, at that very moment, God called Job "blameless and upright." But wait just a minute! Isn't money the root of all evil? And isn't wealth inequality bad? How, therefore, would

God say such a thing? Didn't He know that being super-rich makes a person bad?

Hating "the rich" is an age-old pastime. Our friends and family members may have done it. Figures of speech depict wealth as evil: A man is "filthy rich." A great quantity of possessions is "obscene wealth." Many socialists, if they lived in Job's time, would be crying out to "Soak the rich!" But, does such a perspective align with that of the Bible? And, if we nurture such an attitude toward people who have accumulated wealth, do we reflect God's character? In this chapter, we will consider these questions.

As we shall see, Job was not an outlier, and God does not hate the rich. Nor does He say that wealth is evil or that it is bad to be rich. And He does not command people to hate the rich or to work against them—nor even that it is reasonable or excusable if you do hate them. Let's turn to the Bible to see what it does say about being rich and about rich people.[1]

WEALTH, PROPERLY GAINED AND ENJOYED, IS A BLESSING

Just as a good father will not give his son a snake when he asks for a fish (Matthew 7:10; Luke 11:11), so God will never provide His children with an evil thing, calling it good. The Bible says, "The reward of humility and fear of the LORD are riches, honor and life" (Proverbs 22:4), so we know that riches cannot be evil.

---

1. The words used in the original languages of the Bible related to being rich include עָשִׁיר—'ashir—"rich;" עָשַׁר—ashar—"to be rich;" עָשַׁר—ashshar—"to make rich," עֹשֶׁר—osher—"riches;" שׁוֹעַ—sho'a—"rich, wide, bountiful" (appearing only once, in Job 34:19); הוֹן—hōn—"wealth, substance, riches, sufficiency;" חֹסֶן—chosen—"thing laid up or treasured;" נָשַׂג—nasag—"to reach to, overtake;" חַיִל—chayil—"strength, might, efficiency, wealth, army;" πλούσιος—plousios—"rich," πλουτέω—plouteō—"to be or become rich;" πλουτίζω—ploutizō—"to make rich," and πλοῦτος—ploutos—"riches."

47

The Bible says that wealth and riches will be in the house of the man who fears the LORD and delights in His commandments (Psalm 112:3) and that the LORD makes people rich, bringing them low or exalting them (1 Samuel 2:7). It says an abundance of blessings will come to a faithful man, while someone in a hurry to get rich will be punished (Proverbs 28:20). The Bible calls riches one of the pleasant fruits of the application of wisdom (Proverbs 24:4), and says elsewhere that wisdom holds riches and honor in her left hand (Proverbs 3:16; and enduring wealth, 8:18). Riches are the crown of the wise (Proverbs 14:24), and they come from God (1 Chronicles 29:12, 28).

The Bible says that negligence leads to poverty, but diligence makes one rich; it is the blessing of the LORD that makes rich, "and He adds no sorrow to it" (Proverbs 10:4, 22). It also says that eating and drinking, and enjoying the fruit of one's labor with gladness is a good reward (Ecclesiastes 5:18-20). A working man enjoys pleasant sleep, regardless of how much he eats, but the rich man's sleep is hampered by his full stomach (Ecclesiastes 5:12).

Some men get rich by using dishonest scales (Micah 6:11-12), but wealth should be gained honestly. Everyone will face justice. Those who became rich and fat through injustice are judged by God (Jeremiah 5:26-28), will lose the wealth, and will end up as fools (Jeremiah 17:11).

WHO IS MY NEIGHBOR?

God loves rich people as much as poor people, and he *defends* those of them with whom He is pleased. God said the wealthy Job was blameless and upright, and Psalm 5:12 says, "For it is You who blesses the righteous man, O LORD, You surround him with favor as with a shield."

Throughout the Bible, we encounter wealthy people who pleased God. David, whom God called a man after

His own heart (1 Samuel 13:14), was very wealthy. Solomon pleased God by asking for wisdom to govern God's people instead of riches—and God was pleased to reward him with both (1 Kings 3:11, 13; 2 Chronicles 1:7-12). David's son Solomon became greater than all the kings of the earth in riches and wisdom (1 Kings 10:23-29; 2 Chronicles 9:22), and God allowed him to build the first Temple in Jerusalem.[2] King Jehoshaphat was blessed by God with riches and honor, and he used these to do what was right in God's eyes (2 Chronicles 17:3-5), except in a few matters (2 Chronicles 20:33, 35-37). Likewise, King Hezekiah was blessed with riches and honor (2 Chronicles 32:27). Joseph of Arimathea, a rich man who was also a disciple of Jesus, played a role of honor in his burial (Matthew 27:57-58, Mark 15:43, John 19:38; cf. Isaiah 53:9).

So, there is nothing inherently wrong with being rich, and God has often given great wealth as a reward to those with whom He is pleased. This fact does not mean that God is pleased with everyone who is wealthy, nor that He is displeased with those who are not. "Why do the wicked prosper?" is a fair question (Jeremiah 12:1; Psalm 73:3, 12, 17-18), since dishonest and sinful people often achieve great material prosperity while many who abound in love and good works remain poor.

How, then, are we to act toward rich people? First, we should treat them as people, complete with the same flaws and sinful tendencies as anyone else but also bearing God's image. Just as God does not show partiality (Deuteronomy 10:17; 2 Chronicles 19:7; Acts 10:34; Romans 2:11; Galatians 2:6; Ephesians 6:9), we should favor

---

2. In Solomon's old age, he turned away from God—even building high places for multiple idols of the surrounding peoples. Because of these actions, God tore the kingdom away from him and gave it to his servant. However, the Bible does not attribute Solomon's moral decline to his great wealth, but to his love of many foreign women who then turned his heart away to other gods (I Kings 11:1-8).

neither rich nor poor (Deuteronomy 1:17; Job 34:19; Proverbs 24:23, 28:21; 1 Timothy 5:21). One reason that God's word emphasizes the plight of the poor so much is likely the fact that there exists a natural incentive to favor the rich, while the poor have little to offer. However, preachers of the "social gospel" go out of God's boundaries when they propose favoring the poor and disfavoring the rich. Remember, justice demands an even standard.

WHO IS YOUR MASTER? THE DANGERS OF WEALTH

The Bible contains strong warnings for rich people. These mostly involve *perspective* and *stewardship*. Is wealth a blessing, or a curse? The answer is, "yes." What matters is who owns your heart. If you *serve* wealth, it will become a curse to you. A man with an evil eye hastens after wealth (Proverbs 28:22), and people who want to get rich "fall into temptation and a snare and many harmful desires which plunge men into ruin and destruction" (1 Timothy 6:9). Jesus taught that wealth is deceitful and can cause a man to not be good soil for the work God wants to do in his heart (Matthew 13:22; Mark 4:19; and Luke 8:14). On the other hand, if you serve God with everything He gives you, then the wealth you acquire will be a blessing, regardless of whether it is minor or enormous. Speaking to His disciples, Jesus said,

> "I say to you, make friends for yourselves by means of the wealth of unrighteousness, so that when it fails, they will receive you into the eternal dwellings. He who is faithful in a very little thing is faithful also in much; and he who is unrighteous in a very little thing is unrighteous also in much. Therefore if you have not been faithful in the use of unrighteous wealth, who will entrust the true riches to you? And if you have not been faithful in the use of that which is another's, who will

give you that which is your own? No servant can serve two masters; for either he will hate the one and love the other, or else he will be devoted to one and despise the other. You cannot serve God and wealth." (Luke 16:9-13)

Pay attention to the details. You cannot *serve* God and wealth, and those who *want to get rich* fall into a *temptation and a snare*. These statements do not malign working for profit or possessions, but material prosperity carries some danger. Prosperity also increases our moral obligation to God (Luke 12:48; Matthew 25:14-30). David's injustice against Uriah by stealing his wife and sending him to be killed in battle was made worse in God's eyes by the fact that David was rich, while Uriah was not (2 Samuel 12:1-4).

RIGHT PERSPECTIVE

Clear vision and proper affections help us navigate life. The Bible says a lover of money will not find money satisfying (Ecclesiastes 5:10), and many sacrifice life's joys in pursuit of wealth (Ecclesiastes 4:8). James warned:

> Come now, you who say, "Today or tomorrow we will go to such and such a city, and spend a year there and engage in business and make a profit." Yet you do not know what your life will be like tomorrow. You are just a vapor that appears for a little while and then vanishes away. Instead, you ought to say, "If the Lord wills, we will live and also do this or that." But as it is, you boast in your arrogance; all such boasting is evil. (James 4:13-16)

Years before James wrote those words, Jesus reminded his hearers to keep wealth in perspective with the following story:

"The land of a rich man was very productive. And he began reasoning to himself, saying, 'What shall I do, since I have no place to store my crops?' Then he said, 'This is what I will do: I will tear down my barns and build larger ones, and there I will store all my grain and my goods. And I will say to my soul, "Soul, you have many goods laid up for many years to come; take your ease, eat, drink and be merry."' But God said to him, 'You fool! This very night your soul is required of you; and now who will own what you have prepared?' So is the man who stores up treasure for himself, and is not rich toward God." (Luke 12:16-21)

Notice the details. Similar to the warning James gave, Jesus cautioned against storing up treasure *for ourselves*, while not being rich toward God. The problem was not the man's wealth, but his heart and the actions flowing from it.

Is it possible to have great wealth while also living a life that is pleasing to God? We have already seen many biblical confirmations that it is, but also warnings that wealth can tempt us to wander from God or to neglect the things God wants us to do. The Bible does not state that merely becoming or remaining wealthy is wrong, but it does state that hoarding riches *to the harm of the owner* is a grievous evil; we are born naked and so also will we die, taking none of the fruit of our labors with us (Ecclesiastes 5:13-17). A wise man remembers the difference between the temporal and the eternal. We should learn to be content regardless of our material circumstance; as 1 Timothy 6:6 says, godliness with contentment is great gain. And we should walk with integrity: "Keep deception and lies far from me, give me neither poverty nor riches; feed me with the food that is my portion" (Proverbs 30:8).

To what lengths should you go to become wealthy? Within ethical and moral parameters, part of it has to do with your specific calling; God calls some to business success for His purposes. But as a general principle, King Solomon warned against wearying oneself to gain wealth (Proverbs 23:4). There are things more important than wealth, and high on the list is a good reputation: "A good name is to be more desired than great wealth, favor is better than silver and gold" (Proverbs 22:1). As we saw in the previous chapter, God cares more about a man's heart and his integrity: "Better is the poor who walks in his integrity than he who is crooked though he be rich" (Proverbs 28:6). Righteousness with a little is better than the abundance of many wicked (Psalm 37:16). Riches are fleeting (Job 27:19; Proverbs 27:24).

We should also have a mature perspective on the rich people around us. There is often a mystique that accompanies wealth, but the Bible says not to fear the rich man, for he will soon perish, taking nothing with him (Psalm 49:16-20). Riches are no help against death and no help in redeeming a soul; rich and poor alike will soon be gone (Psalm 49:1-12). Riches do not profit on the day of wrath (Proverbs 11:4). He who trusts in riches will fall (Proverbs 11:28). The rich man should glory in his low position, because he will pass away like the grass, even while he goes about his business (James 1:10-11).

So, what should you do if you are rich, or if you are becoming so? Hebrews 11:24-26 says that Moses considered the reproach of Christ and enduring ill-treatment with the people of God to be greater riches than the treasures of Egypt. If your riches increase, then, do not set your heart on them (Psalm 62:10). If you are rich in this world, don't be conceited and don't fix your hope upon the uncertainty of riches, but on God (1 Timothy 6:17). If you trust in your riches and will not make God your refuge, you will be laughed at by the righteous (Psalm 52:7). Jesus said that where your treasure is, there your heart will be also (Matthew 6:21), and your heart should be with God:

Thus says the LORD, "Let not a wise man boast of his wisdom, and let not the mighty man boast of his might, let not a rich man boast of his riches; but let him who boasts boast of this, that he understands and knows Me, that I am the LORD who exercises lovingkindness, justice and righteousness on earth; for I delight in these things," declares the LORD. (Jeremiah 9:23-24)

So, in addition to righteousness, justice, and lovingkindness (*ḥeṣed*), we should be humble even if we become rich. Paul wrote similarly,

Instruct those who are rich in this present world not to be conceited or to fix their hope on the uncertainty of riches, but on God, who richly supplies us with all things to enjoy. Instruct them to do good, to be rich in good works, to be generous and ready to share, storing up for themselves the treasure of a good foundation for the future, so that they may take hold of that which is life indeed. (1 Timothy 6:17-19)

We conclude this section with two teachings of Jesus that should remind us to attend with urgency to eternal matters, above riches and the comforts that accompany them in this life. In the first, Jesus said, "Woe to you rich, for you are receiving your comfort in full. Woe to you who are well-fed now, for you shall be hungry. Woe to you who laugh now, for you shall mourn and weep. Woe to you when all men speak well of you, for their fathers used to treat the false prophets in the same way" (Luke 6:24-26).

Second, in Luke 16:19-31, Jesus told a story about an un-named rich man, and a poor man named Lazarus. The rich man made a habit of dressing lavishly, and he lived daily in joyous splendor. The poor Lazarus was laid at the rich man's gate, covered with sores, wishing to even be fed with the crumbs falling from the rich man's table, and the dogs were licking his sores. Both men died, whereupon Lazarus was taken to "Abraham's bosom," while the rich man found himself tormented by fire in Hades, from where he cried out, asking Abraham to send Lazarus to give him even a little relief. Abraham, however, reminded the rich man that he had good things during his life, that now Lazarus was being comforted, and that there was now an uncrossable chasm fixed between them.

CAN A RICH MAN ENTER THE KINGDOM OF GOD?

There was a time when Jesus gave a very difficult instruction to a rich young ruler, and then made a sobering statement. Let's look at it:

> A ruler questioned Him, saying, "Good Teacher, what shall I do to inherit eternal life?" And Jesus said to him, "Why do you call Me good? No one is good except God alone. You know the commandments, 'Do not commit adultery, Do not murder, Do not steal, Do not bear false witness, Honor your father and mother.'" And he said, "All these things I have kept from my youth." When Jesus heard this, He said to him, "One thing you still lack; sell all that you possess and distribute it to the poor, and you shall have treasure in heaven; and come, follow Me." But when he had heard these things, he became very sad, for he was extremely rich. And Jesus looked at him and said, "How hard it is for those who are wealthy to enter the kingdom of God! For it is easier for a camel to go through the eye of a needle than for a rich man to enter the kingdom of God." They who heard it said, "Then who can be saved?" But He said, "The things that are impossible with people are possible with God." (Luke 18:18-27; cf. Matthew 19:16-26 and Mark 10:17-27)

At first glance, Jesus' teaching seems to spell doom for all rich people. But look at how His hearers responded. They did not say *it's a good thing I'm not rich*, but rather *Then who can be saved?* It was a very astute question. They did not hear Jesus saying that only people richer than they would have great difficulty entering heaven. They understood that *everyone* is rich and therefore faces this enormous challenge. And Jesus answered, "What is impossible with men is possible with God."

Why did Jesus tell this young man to go sell everything? Does that mean that it was immoral for him to have possessions? Not necessarily. But the question helped to show the young man a problem in his own heart: he placed his love of riches above his love for God. In Luke 19, we read of another rich man, named Zacchaeus, who was freed from love of money when he followed Jesus and pledged to make restitution to those he had previously cheated.

We conclude this section with one last passage, a severe warning from the book of James:

> Come now, you rich, weep and howl for your miseries which are coming upon you. Your riches have rotted and your garments have become moth-eaten. Your gold and your silver have rusted; and their rust will be a witness against you and will consume your flesh like fire. It is in the last days that you have stored up your treasure! Behold, the pay of the laborers who mowed your fields, and which has been withheld by you, cries out against you; and the outcry of those who did the harvesting has reached the ears of the Lord of Sabaoth. You have lived luxuriously on the earth and led a life of wanton pleasure; you have fattened your hearts in a day of slaughter. You have condemned and put to death the righteous man; he does not resist you. (James 5:1-6)

Toward whom were James' warnings directed? All

rich people? No, just those rich people who withheld the agreed-upon pay from the laborers (cf. Matthew 20:1-16), while living lavishly and in pursuit of pleasure, or who condemned and put to death the righteous. In the accusation about storing up treasure in the last days, we also discern a sin of omission. The gold and silver accumulated by the accused at a time when the Lord's return was imminent and when these materials might have been applied to some profitable work for God's kingdom.

SOCIALIST MISUNDERSTANDINGS

Socialists commonly assume that rich people must be greedy, and that poor people aren't. Neither is categorically true. Poverty does not make one immune from temptation, and one need not be rich to love money or be greedy. Indeed, socialism is driven by greed, fear, and jealousy among those hoping to enrich themselves without the consent of those from whom wealth will be seized.

One misconception that proponents of socialism use to build resentment against rich people is what is often called the fallacy of the fixed pie. There are people who suppose that there is a limited amount of wealth to be had in the world or in any local area. If that were true, then one person having more wealth would mean there is less to go around for everyone else.

In the real world, however, there can hardly exist such a thing as a limited-goods (also known as "fixed pie" or "zero sum") economy because human ingenuity and industry are the limiting factors in almost every instance, not the resources available. But even supposing—for the sake of argument—that a fixed pie model was correct, would such a reality mean that some people having more than others is wrong according to a biblical standard? The answer, from a biblical perspective, would still be no.

In contrast to the materialism of socialists who divide people into victims and oppressors until all wealth is "equitably" distributed, God reminds us again and again that wealth is ultimately neither the source of our happiness nor our security in life. It is true in a way that the rich man's wealth is his fortress (Proverbs 10:15) and his strong city (Proverbs 18:11), and many people love the rich (Proverbs 14:20). But whether rich or poor, anyone is foolish who puts ultimate trust in his wealth, since all will die and leave it to others, while it is God who redeems a soul from the power of the grave (Psalm 49:15).

CHAPTER SUMMARY

God called Job, the wealthiest man of the east, "my servant" and presented him as the highest moral example of his day. There are many others in the Bible who are not blamed for their great wealth. The Bible says riches are a reward for hard work, wisdom, and fear of the LORD. So, although there are dangers to the soul associated with wealth, there is nothing inherently wrong about being extremely rich—and anyone who says otherwise calls God a liar. Rather, whether we are wealthy, poor, or somewhere in between, we should be generous and humble, place our trust in God and not riches, and do good.

CHAPTER 6

The Ten Commandments

The earth is the LORD's, and everything in it, the world, and all who live in it. (Psalm 24:1)

E verything we have is a gift from God and ultimately belongs to Him, and our evaluation of economic systems must keep that fact in mind. Your life, health, and property only exist because He created them and upholds them moment by moment by the word of His power (Hebrews 1:3).

Yet, affirmation of property ownership permeates God's commandments concerning the way we are to live in society. And, when it comes to man's place in creation, God made clear His intention that men and women are to be in authority on earth. Far from being a mere concession or necessary evil, our dominion over nature is—according to the Bible—central to God's design and purpose:

"Be fruitful and multiply, and fill the earth, and subdue it; and rule over the fish of the sea and over the birds of the sky and over every living thing that moves on the earth ... Behold, I have given you every plant yielding seed that is on the surface of all the earth, and every tree which has fruit yielding seed; it shall be food for you; and to every beast of the earth and to every bird of the sky and to every thing that moves on the earth which has life, I have given every green plant for food." (Genesis 1:28-31)

Notice that these words represent God's statement of man's *purpose* and proper *role* on this earth that He created. First, we are to be fruitful and multiply. This means having children—lots of them. Unless God has specifically told you otherwise, having children, as God gives them, is never a sin. Rather, it is a command from God, Who made you and the world in which you live.

Second, we are to fill the earth. That's right, we are supposed to spread out and occupy every corner of this planet that we are able. Again, doing so is a command from God. And, not only are we to *fill* the earth; we are also to *subdue* it. That is, clearly, we are to cultivate and bring order to every part of the earth. The scope of this command probably includes, but is not limited to, taming animals, farming and harvesting fields, building homes and other structures, inventing and manufacturing useful items, and so forth. And yes, I believe it means (since we are created in God's image, Genesis 1:27) that we are to be engaged in creative activities such as invention and the arts.

Is your "carbon footprint" a concern? Re-read Genesis 1:28-31, and I believe that you will find the answer to be "absolutely not!"—so long as the 'carbon footprint' is the result of your being fruitful and multiplying, filling the earth, and subduing it. Your breathing, driving, farming, building, settling, multiplying, living on a tract of land, and traveling from place to place is precisely what God told all of us to be doing. Anyone who leads you to feel guilty—about existing, about breathing, about your use of resources, about your water consumption or your burning of wood or other fuel, or your defecation or trash disposal, or anything else about your ordinary activity that does not expressly violate a moral commandment from God—is not speaking on God's behalf. Do not listen to that person. We are surrounded by people who do not have the mind of God and who do not represent His will for us. Tune them out and turn your eyes back to God.

THE TEN COMMANDMENTS

In the third month after Moses led the people of Israel out of slavery in Egypt, God called Moses up to Mount Sinai and gave him the Ten Commandments. These were His words:

> "I am the LORD your God, who brought you out of the land of Egypt, out of the house of slavery.
>
> "You shall have no other gods before Me.
>
> "You shall not make for yourself an idol, or any likeness of what is in heaven above or on the earth beneath or in the water under the earth. You shall not worship them or serve them; for I, the LORD your God, am a jealous God, visiting the iniquity of the fathers on the children, on the third and the fourth generations of those who hate Me, but showing lovingkindness to thousands, to those who love Me and keep My commandments.
>
> "You shall not take the name of the LORD your God in vain, for the LORD will not leave him unpunished who takes His name in vain.
>
> "Remember the sabbath day, to keep it holy. Six days you shall labor and do all your work, but the seventh day is a sabbath of the LORD your God; in it you shall not do any work, you or your son or your daughter, your male or your female servant or your cattle or

your sojourner who stays with you. For in six days the LORD made the heavens and the earth, the sea and all that is in them, and rested on the seventh day; therefore the LORD blessed the sabbath day and made it holy.

"Honor your father and your mother, that your days may be prolonged in the land which the LORD your God gives you.

"You shall not murder.

"You shall not commit adultery.

"You shall not steal.

"You shall not bear false witness against your neighbor.

"You shall not covet your neighbor's house; you shall not covet your neighbor's wife or his male servant or his female servant or his ox or his donkey or anything that belongs to your neighbor." (Exodus 20:2-17)

The first four commandments address our relationship with God, and the last six have to do with our relationship with others. In some sense, the last six commandments are all prohibitions against theft: the fifth forbids stealing the honor due your parents, the sixth forbids stealing another's life through murder, the seventh forbids stealing another's sole right to intimacy with his or her spouse, the eighth forbids literal stealing, the ninth forbids theft of another's name or right to justice, and the tenth forbids what might be called the premeditation of theft.

At least two of the commandments protect other people's tangible possessions. We are not to steal (Exodus 20:15), and we are not to covet (Exodus 20:17). According to these, blame lies with the one who covets, the one who fails to take joy in a neighbor's prosperity, and not with the one who owns the things coveted or stolen. These prohibitions are expressions of the second greatest commandment, to love our neighbor as we love ourselves (Leviticus 19:18, Matthew 22:39).

IS MONEY EVIL?

Some believe the Bible says "money is the root of all evil." The King James Version notwithstanding, it does not. In 1 Timothy 6:10, Paul writes, "For the love of money is a root of all sorts of evil, and some by longing for it have wandered away from the faith and pierced themselves with many griefs." It does not say money is evil, nor even that its love is the lone root of anything, but that *love* of money is *a* root of *all sorts* (that is, various types) of evil. So, God's word in this verse calls attention to an *attitude of the heart* toward money, not the mere fact of its existence, nor even its accumulation.

As discussed in Chapter 5, we know that accumulating wealth is not categorically bad from the example of Job, from the Bible's many references to God rewarding some people with great wealth, from the fourth ("Six days you shall labor"), eighth ("You shall not steal"), and tenth ("You shall not covet") commandments, and from passages like Proverbs 6:6-11:

> Go to the ant, O sluggard, observe her ways and be wise, which having no chief, officer or ruler, prepares her food in the summer, and gathers her provisions in the harvest. How long will you lie down, O sluggard? When will you arise from your sleep? "A little sleep, a little slumber, a little folding of the hands to rest"— your poverty will come in like a vagabond and your need like an armed man.

So, we ought to take initiative, be industrious, and accumulate wealth: these activities are *wise*! Moral problems arise only when a property owner does not keep it in right perspective, or when it becomes a tool for injustice or immoral activity. Apart from that, ownership of property is a part of our lives fully affirmed by God as good and something to be sought, so long as it does not become an idol.

There is another passage related to the accumulation of possessions that carries potential for misapplication. It is found among Jesus' instructions to His disciples:

> And as you go, preach, saying, 'The kingdom of heaven is at hand.' Heal the sick, raise the dead, cleanse the lepers, cast out demons. Freely you received, freely give. Do not acquire gold, or silver, or copper for your money belts, or a bag for your journey, or even two coats, or sandals, or a staff; for the worker is worthy of his support. (Matthew 10:7-10)

Should no one own anything but the clothes on his back and the items he can carry? No, because that would contradict many other sections of the Bible, such as "Go to the ant." No, these were instructions to Jesus' disciples, for a specific purpose, time of their lives, and mission. They were being sent to preach. It was not a principle for all people, or even a command to all Christians. There is great wisdom, however, in Jesus' instruction to give freely. A person who trusts God will generally hold possessions lightly and practice generosity, knowing that those things are a temporary gift from God in the first place.

So, where have we come on the topic of property and ownership? First, we are not imposters on this earth. We are the ones to whom God has given a command to fill and subdue it. Second, as we saw in the Ten Commandments, and will see even more fully in coming chapters, we are to respect the property of others by not stealing and not coveting. And finally, we should keep a right perspective on the property that we own—that is to say, that which God has entrusted to our individual stewardship.

CHAPTER SUMMARY

God's command not to steal or covet confirms the right of your neighbor to own property and to dispose of it as he wishes. It also confirms that anyone seeking to redistribute wealth or other property without consent from the owner is engaged in doing evil. Jesus' command to His disciples not to acquire gold, silver, or duplicate items of clothing was not a universal one, but rather a specific instruction tailored to their particular task and purpose. We should all remember that our time on earth is limited, and while we ought to remain industrious, we should also keep a good perspective and not put our trust in possessions.

CHAPTER 7

Work

S peaking of being industrious, why does God—
Who made everything and to Whom we are like
grasshoppers (Isaiah 40:22)—care if we work? Why
does it matter to Him whether you wake up in the
morning and do something productive with your time
and energy? Does God need our productivity? Does our
labor at any task give Him something that He could not
merely speak into existence?

The obvious answer is "no," yet God repeatedly and
explicitly tells us to *work*. In fact, our work is so important to Him that it is the subject of the Fourth Commandment:

> "Six days you shall labor and do all your work ... For in
> six days the LORD made the heavens and the earth, the
> sea and all that is in them" (Exodus 20:9, 11; cf.
> Deuteronomy 5:13-14)

Socialism rests upon a very different view of the
meaning and purpose of work from that of the Bible.
Near the end of this chapter, after we have surveyed what

the Bible says, we will briefly discuss the socialist view and allow the stark contrast to become evident. Remember, the question we ask is not whether the Bible must dictate secular laws, but whether socialism is right according to a biblical standard—that is, whether those who follow God can rightly support it.

THE MEANING OF WORK

God says to work six days of the week, because He worked six days when He made everything. Because we are made in God's image, He says, it is right for us to follow that pattern. For six days each week, work is right. On one day of the week, the sabbath, work becomes sin.

Work, then, has spiritual meaning. There are different types of work (e.g., pastor, nanny, president, brick-layer, janitor, farmer, cook, salesperson, etc.), and we might imagine ours is not important. Such a notion should be resisted. Paul reminded the Colossians that even menial work honors God: "Whatever you do, do your work heartily, as for the Lord rather than for men, knowing that from the Lord you will receive the reward of the in-heritance" (Colossians 3:23-24). Of course, some work is illicit or immoral, and we must not make God's command to work into an excuse for doing things the Bible calls sin.

Work *always* results in profit. "In all labor there is profit, but mere talk leads only to poverty" (Proverbs 14:23). Profit can be material or immaterial, good (Titus 3:8) or bad (e.g., Romans 6:23, "the wages of sin is death"). Proverbs 3:14, says wisdom's profit—evidently not merely physical—is *better* than that of silver or fine gold. When you do your work, remember that there is profit beyond what is visible in a paycheck or a bank account.

Material profit can be saved, enjoyed, given away, or put to work for some purpose or another. Unfortunately, it can sometimes be stolen by others or devoured by circumstance, such as rust, moths, or natural disaster. Ultimately, all our material profits will turn to dust (Ecclesiastes 3:20), so a wise person will not neglect to give attention to other types of profit. As Jesus said, "What will it profit a man if he gains the whole world and forfeits his soul? Or what will a man give in exchange for his soul?" (Matthew 16:26; cf. Mark 8:36 and Luke 9:25)

Work should make up a large part of our activity, but it should not be without end. In fact, the punishment for work on the sabbath was to be *death* (Exodus 31:14-15; 35:2). A full discussion of the sabbath, Saturday, and work on the first day (the Lord's Day, that is, Sunday) through Friday since Jesus' death and resurrection, is beyond the scope of this book, but both sabbath and Jubilee (to be discussed in Chapter 14) were fulfilled in Jesus, Who is the Thing itself while they are but shadows of Him (Colossians 2:16-17). Christians acknowledge the sabbath, though some (following the example of the early church, who began to worship on the first day of the week) mistakenly conflate the Old Testament's sabbath with Sunday, while others incorrectly imagine sabbath observance to play a role in their salvation. It does not (Romans 3:20, 28; Ephesians 2:8-9).

THE REASON FOR WORK

"Because I said so" should be reason enough to obey our parents. Since God said to work, we should work. But God is a good Father, and the commandments—including the commandment to work—are for our good and not our harm. Work is hard, rather than pure joy, because of Adam and Eve's sin: "Cursed is the ground because of you; in toil you will eat of it all the days of your life. Both thorns and thistles it shall grow for you; and you will eat the plants of the field; by the sweat of your face you will eat bread, till you return to the ground" (Genesis 3:17-19).

One purpose for work is our own provision. We have already seen that there is profit in all labor, and that we should follow the example of the ant who works and saves. We should not work half-heartedly, but should do our best: Diligence brings wealth, and negligence poverty (Proverbs 10:4); slack work brings destruction (Proverbs 18:9), the desire of the sluggard who refuses to work puts him to death (Proverbs 21:25), and love of pleasure will make one poor (Proverbs 21:17). The Bible says we should be willing to work for our own sustenance (2 Thessalonians 3:10-12). Jesus' disciples did honest work as fishermen (Luke 5:2-5; cf. John 21:7-8).

God promises to establish the plans of those who commit their works to Him (Proverbs 16:3), and that the one skilled in his work will stand before kings (Proverbs 22:29). And He rewards the hard worker with pleasant sleep (Ecclesiastes 5:12). The Proverbs 31 woman is praised for—among many other things—her diligence and the joy she takes in her good works (Proverbs 31:13, 31). Our work in this life should be kept in perspective. God tells us to do work, but the Bible also says that all the works we do are vanity and striving after the wind (Ecclesiastes 1:14, 2:17, 3:9). On the day of the Lord, the earth and all its works will be burned up (2 Peter 3:10).

Sometimes menial work brings opportunities we would not otherwise have (Acts 18:3). Our work should not be merely for ourselves, but to enable us to be generous toward others (Acts 20:35). Non-transactional work is also important (Romans 16:3, 6, 9, 12, 21; Philippians 4:3; Colossians 1:29; 1 Thessalonians 2:9; 5:12-13; 1 Timothy 5:10; 6:18; Titus 2:5). Ultimately, we are made for work, and we need to work—to experience the joy of producing some outcome or product. To deny an able person such satisfaction by making him entitled to sustenance on the backs of his neighbors is to rob him of part of his humanity.

THE SOCIALIST CONCEPT OF WORK

The motto of Hitler's National Socialists was *Arbeit Macht Frei* "work sets you free." Marx' and Engels' *Communist Manifesto* begins, "Workers of the world, unite!" Work is a central motif of the socialist enterprise—but the meaning and outcome of work to a socialist is very different from that laid out in the Bible. For one thing, socialists see no essential claim for the worker to even his own labor. Labor and its fruits belong to the collective, not to himself—this is why the socialist justifies both slavery and wealth redistribution (we will return to this topic in Chapter 15). Socialists love workers in the abstract, but divorce them in reality from work's meaning and deny the worker any essential claim to his effort or its product.

CHAPTER SUMMARY

God made us, male and female, in His image. He made us for a purpose, to fill the earth and subdue it. Part of being in His image, with this specific task of filling and subduing the earth, is *work*, which—in the fourth commandment—He directs us to do six days out of the week. In all work, the Bible tells us there is profit. Because we are made to work, and to take joy in our work and its results, for anyone to divorce our work from its results, or to take the results from us against our will, is a theft of something that we need as men and women.

CHAPTER 8

The Acts Church

A cts 5 contains one of the clearest moral
affirmations of property ownership to be found
anywhere in the Bible. So, it really is amazing that
some have tried to present it as evidence that God favors
socialism. As usual, the false view is exposed upon a closer
look at the details.

It would be wrong to suggest that the main lesson to
be drawn from the Acts church is the justice of free markets and property. That observation is only incidental.
However, to insist that the scenario means the opposite—
that it denies the individual's moral right to his or her
property—would require us to either ignore Peter's words
or remove them from the Bible. We will do neither.

Let us, then, lay out the scene before looking carefully
to understand exactly what God affirms as moral—and
what He rejects as wrong. The setting is Jerusalem during
the months following Jesus' death and resurrection, and
immediately after the outpouring of the Holy Spirit on
the day of Pentecost. Peter had made his powerful speech,
and three thousand people were added in a single day to
the initial number of about one hundred and twenty, and

were baptized. This early church was zealous and united as one family. It was a very special moment. Such unity among all believers has probably never been seen before nor since. It must have been wonderful to see and experience.

We read that those who believed during this time "were together and had all things in common; and they began selling their property and possessions and were sharing them with all, as anyone might have need. Day by day continuing with one mind in the temple, and breaking bread from house to house, they were taking their meals together with gladness and sincerity of heart, praising God and having favor with all the people. And the Lord was adding to their number day by day those who were being saved" (Acts 2:44-47). Eventually, "not one of them claimed that anything belonging to him was his own, but all things were common property to them" (Acts 4:32). Believers were selling their houses and land, and bringing the proceeds to lay at the apostles' feet to administer and distribute as they saw fit. Although the text does not state that they were clustered into one space, rather than living throughout Jerusalem, it would not be incorrect to characterize their mode of life as communal, in the sense of holding property in common.

Among the Jerusalem believers were a property-owning husband and wife. After Barnabas sold a tract of land he owned and brought the money to the apostles, it seems that this couple, possibly motivated by guilt or a desire for social approval, did something similar. Let's pick up the biblical account here:

A man named Ananias, with his wife Sapphira, sold a piece of property, and kept back some of the price for himself, with his wife's full knowledge, and bringing a portion of it, he laid it at the apostles' feet. But Peter said, "Ananias, why has Satan filled your heart to lie to the Holy Spirit and to keep back some of the price of the land? While it remained unsold, did it not remain your own? And after it was sold, was it not under your control? Why is it that you have conceived this deed in your heart? You have not lied to men but to God." And as he heard these words, Ananias fell down and breathed his last; and great fear came over all who heard of it. The young men got up and covered him up, and after carrying him out, they buried him.

Now there elapsed an interval of about three hours, and his wife came in, not knowing what had happened. And Peter responded to her, "Tell me whether you sold the land for such and such a price?" And she said, "Yes, that was the price." Then Peter said to her, "Why is it that you have agreed together to put the Spirit of the Lord to the test? Behold, the feet of those who have buried your husband are at the door, and they will carry you out as well." And immediately she fell at his feet and breathed her last, and the young men came in and found her dead, and they carried her out and buried her beside her husband. (Acts 5:1-10)

So, what happened? At first glance, one might get the impression that Peter was angry at Ananias for failing to give Peter all the money from the sale of his property. But, that is not what Peter said. In fact, Peter confirmed to Ananias that it was up to him whether to sell the land in the first place, and it was also up to him whether to lay the whole amount at the apostles' feet or not. What Peter faulted Ananias for was *lying to God*. Ananias represented the amount he gave as though it were the entire sale price of his field. The same scene is repeated with his wife Sapphira, who also lied to Peter about the sale price.

Were Ananias and Sapphira compelled by the apostles or anyone else to sell their property? No. After they had sold their property, were Ananias and Sapphira forced to hand the money to Peter? Again, no. Social pressure certainly existed, but Ananias' decision to bring money to

Peter was voluntary. These two were not struck dead by God for failing to share all their possessions. Even in Jerusalem, there was no general mandate or command from God or the apostles for believers—let alone secular society—to liquidate their possessions or to hand them over to common administration by leaders.

In fact, even during this time period, individual responsibility for needs was emphasized: "If anyone does not provide for his own, and especially for those of his household, he has denied the faith and is worse than an unbeliever ... if any woman who is a believer has dependent widows, she must assist them" (1 Timothy 5:8, 16).

In 2 Corinthians 8:1-4, Paul reported how the believers in Macedonia overflowed with generosity despite their biting poverty. He held them up as an example, writing to the Corinthians,

> "See that you abound in this gracious work also. I am not speaking this as a command, but as proving through the earnestness of others the sincerity of your love also ... For if the readiness is present, it is acceptable according to what a person has, not according to what he does not have. For this is not for the ease of others and for your affliction, but by way of equality—at this present time your abundance being a supply for their need, so that their abundance also may become a supply for your need, that there may be equality; as it is written, 'HE WHO GATHERED MUCH DID NOT HAVE TOO MUCH, AND HE WHO GATHERED LITTLE HAD NO LACK'"(2 Corinthians 8:7–8, 12-15).

The final part of this passage is a quotation from Exodus 16:18 and refers to Israel's gathering of the manna that God sent down daily for them in the wilderness. All that we gather through our labors are gifts from God: "Every good thing given and every perfect gift is from above, coming down from the Father of lights, with whom there is no variation or shifting shadow" (James 1:17). But here, as elsewhere, Paul assumes his hearers own their property—that is why he urges them to practice love and good stewardship.

Imagine for a moment what the instruction of the Acts church or Paul might have been if they had a socialist premise. Their command would have been to recognize a right of the leaders—or of secular government—to redistribute resources, and for everyone to just go along with it. If Karl Marx had written the Bible, that is what we would expect to see. But it is not what we find in these passages, or anywhere else in the Bible.

CHAPTER SUMMARY

The early Jerusalem church voluntarily held their possessions in common, administered by the apostles. There was no order for everyone in Jerusalem to divest themselves of their property and place it into hands of the secular governing authorities, nor even a command for the believers to do so. The giving was by the believers, to the apostles, as an act of love for God and toward the advance of the Gospel. There is no indication in scripture that what happened then is a mandate or perpetual model for the church, much less a viable practice for secular society.

CHAPTER 9

The Parable of the Workers in the Vineyard

Is it fair for an employer to pay workers different hourly rates for the same job? Some people today would emphatically answer, "No! Anything other than equal work for equal pay is unfair and unjust!" But would you be surprised to find that their view goes against what the Bible says?

Jesus Himself emphasized that different pay rates are entirely just, so long as they are the result of mutual agreement between employer and employee. The Parable of the Workers in the Vineyard, found in Matthew 20, is one of many clear biblical affirmations of everyone's right to do as he wishes with his property. Let's take a look.

Jesus once took an opportunity to teach His disciples how the kingdom of heaven works. Peter had just asked Him a question about how he and his fellow disciples would be taken care of in heaven in relation to others who were following the Lord. In answer, Jesus told Peter plainly that the twelve disciples would sit on twelve thrones judging the twelve tribes of Israel, and also that there would be rewards many times greater than what they had left behind for "everyone who has left houses or brothers or sisters or father or mother or children or farms" for His name's sake (Matthew 19:29). But Jesus tempered Peter's expectations with a further statement that many who are first will be last, while the last will be first—and this statement constituted Jesus' transition to the parable that we will now consider.

Jesus often taught in parables—stories that employ relatable examples modeled on real life situations to illustrate deep truths. As the teacher, Jesus could choose the story. As we will see, His evident purpose at this moment was to show how God's decision to show mercy and generosity was *God's right* and *perfectly just*. What sort of story do you suppose He picked?

We don't need to imagine. Thanks to Matthew's written record of these events, we can read what Jesus said. This passage is often titled the "Parable of the Workers in the Vineyard," and it is one of the most powerful demonstrations that what we today call capitalism or free market exchange is a just system when measured by God's standard. Here is the parable:

> "For the kingdom of heaven is like a landowner who went out early in the morning to hire laborers for his vineyard. When he had agreed with the laborers for a denarius for the day, he sent them into his vineyard. And he went out about the third hour and saw others standing idle in the market place; and to those he said, 'You also go into the vineyard, and whatever is right I will give you.' And so they went. Again he went out about the sixth and the ninth hour, and did the same thing. And about the eleventh hour he went out and found others standing around; and he said to them, 'Why have you been standing here idle all day long?' They said to him, 'Because no one hired us.' He said to them, 'You go into the vineyard too.'
>
> "When evening came, the owner of the vineyard said to his foreman, 'Call the laborers and pay them

their wages, beginning with the last group to the first.' When those hired about the eleventh hour came, each one received a denarius. When those hired first came, they thought that they would receive more; but each of them also received a denarius. When they received it, they grumbled at the landowner, saying, 'These last men have worked only one hour, and you have made them equal to us who have borne the burden and the scorching heat of the day.' But he answered and said to one of them, 'Friend, I am doing you no wrong; did you not agree with me for a denarius? Take what is yours and go, but I wish to give to this last man the same as to you. Is it not lawful for me to do what I wish with what is my own? Or is your eye envious because I am generous?' So the last shall be first, and the first last." (Matthew 20:1-16)

Let's discuss the contents of this passage. What happened? A landowner needed workers to harvest his vineyard. He went out and offered a certain amount of pay—one denarius—for a day's work. Some men accepted the offer and were sent into the vineyard to work. Later, about 9 a.m., he did the same and added more workers. He did the same again, around noon, then around 3 p.m., and finally at 5 p.m. The end of the work day was 6 p.m., and the owner called the last workers hired, who had worked only one hour, to collect their pay. When he gave them each a denarius, the exact amount he had agreed to pay those hired first, the others began to expect more. However, they were disappointed—not because the owner failed to keep his promise, but because they were jealous, and their adjusted expectations turned out to not be true. He paid them just as they had agreed, and upon their protestation, he pointed out that he had done them no wrong by being more generous to other workers with whom he had made a different arrangement.

The main principles laid out by Jesus are, first, the

owner has the right to do as he pleases with what he owns; second, a contract between two parties justly governs their working arrangement; and third, coveting the property of others is wrong.

Now, let's recognize what the parable was about. From the context, we understand that Jesus did not tell it with the main purpose of teaching about justice in human economic interactions. Rather, He used a situation that could exist in the lives of His hearers as a means of helping them understand something about the kingdom of heaven.

However, even though economic interactions between people was not the *primary* lesson Jesus was teaching in the Parable of the Workers in the Vineyard, we can notice in this story what God presents as just in human economic relationships. That these are all in harmony with teachings found in the rest of the Bible concerning justice in economic interactions confirms that we are not reading into the passage.

To understand the moral weight of the matter, let us first agree that Jesus would never portray God's actions as *unjust*. The Bible is clear that God is just. For example, Job 8:3 asks, "Does God pervert justice? Or does the Almighty pervert what is right?"—these are rhetorical questions, with the obvious answer being "no." In Psalm 51:4, David says to God, "You are justified when You speak and blameless when You judge." Meanwhile, in Psalm 89:14, Ethan the Ezrahite says to God, "Righteousness and justice are the foundation of Your throne" (a similar phrase recurs in Psalm 97:2). And in Psalm 111:7, we read that "the works of His hands are truth and justice; all His precepts are sure." Isaiah 30:18 tells us, "The LORD is a God of justice; How blessed are all those who long for Him." And, in Jeremiah 9:24 God says, "I am the LORD who exercises lovingkindness, justice and righteousness on earth; for I delight in these things."

Therefore, we must understand that the actions of the

landlord in this parable—who is meant to represent God —are *just,* and that therefore, contractual agreements of differing terms between freely consenting parties are also inherently just.

CHAPTER SUMMARY

When Jesus illustrated God's justice in admitting people to heaven at a late hour and without works in Matthew 20:1-16, He chose an example of an employer-employee relationship in which the workers complained about differing hourly rates. Jesus invited His hearers to recognize the justice of a contract mutually agreed, the right of the landowner to be selectively generous with his wealth, and the sin of coveting. Since God is just, it would have made no sense for Jesus to use an example of human injustice as a model for God's dealings with men. Therefore, we must assume that the payment of differing hourly wages of whatever amount, if mutually agreed by all parties from the beginning, is inherently fair.

CHAPTER 10

Two Tunics and a Neighbor in Need

In April of 2020, Pope Francis—who had lately been calling for forced wealth redistribution in the form of a universal basic wage—delivered a sermon in Rome urging the elimination of inequalities, saying, "This is not some ideology, it is Christianity." He also pressed his hearers to use the COVID-19 pandemic "as an opportunity to prepare for our collective future," and seemed to suggest that God Himself would not be able to preserve the future for *anyone* unless there is "an all-embracing vision."[1]

Socialists tend to operate on an assumption that uneven distribution of wealth is unfair, and they occasionally bring forward selected parts of the Bible in alleged support for that claim. But does the Bible really state that possessions should be leveled? If you have read this far, you probably understand that the answer is *no*. In this chapter, we consider a Bible passage sometimes presented

1. Winfield, Nicole, "Pope dreams of post-virus world where inequalities abolished." Associated Press, April 19, 2020.

in support of wealth leveling. Speaking to the crowds one day, John the Baptist said,

> "You brood of vipers, who warned you to flee from the wrath to come? Therefore bear fruit in keeping with repentance ... Indeed the axe is already laid at the root of the trees; so every tree that does not bear good fruit is cut down and thrown into the fire." And the crowds were questioning him, saying, "Then what shall we do?" And he would answer and say to them, "The man who has two tunics is to share with him who has none; and he who has food is to do likewise." (Luke 3:7-11)

First, the speaker is Jesus' first cousin, John. Second, his statement, "the man who has two tunics is to share with him who has none; and he who has food is to do likewise"—came in response to the crowd asking John what they should do to avert the axe that he said was already laid at the root of the trees, ready to cut down and throw into the fire every one that does not bear good fruit.

Now, John was obviously telling his hearers to do good, not evil. When one man has a surplus and another is on the brink of starvation or dangerous exposure to the elements or public shame from nakedness, it is right for him who has extra to share with him, to avert the immediate danger. Saving a stranger from real harm or shame is a simple and obvious application of Luke 6:31, "Treat others the same way you want them to treat you."

Second, John said to *share*. The Greek is μεταδότω *metadotó*, which means "to share with someone else what one has."[2] It is used in a similar sense in Ephesians 4:28, "that he will have [something] **to share** with one... ." The

---

2. Luow, Johannes P. and Eugene A. Nida, *Greek-English lexicon of the New Testament: based on semantic domains* (New York: the United Bible Societies, 1988). Volume I. 569.

word can also mean to give (e.g., charitably), as in Romans 12:6-8, or to impart, as in Romans 1:11, "that I may **impart** some spiritual gift to you," or 1 Thessalonians 2:8, "Having so fond an affection for you, we were well-pleased to **impart** to you not only the gospel of God but also our own lives, because you had become very dear to us."

Finally, notice the *voluntary* nature of the act. John was telling people who had asked him what they should do to avoid God's impending wrath: He "is to" (KJV "Let the one who") share of his own free will with those in great need. The word is gentle and generally uncompelled.

The foundation for individual obligation to a neighbor in need runs throughout the Old Testament. As with John the Baptist's instructions to the crowds who wanted to escape God's wrath, so also God's instructions to the people of Israel were *specific*, *personal*, and *limited*:

> When you make your neighbor a loan of any sort, you shall not enter his house to take his pledge. You shall remain outside, and the man to whom you make the loan shall bring the pledge out to you. If he is a poor man, you shall not sleep with his pledge. When the sun goes down you shall surely return the pledge to him, that he may sleep in his cloak and bless you; and it will be righteousness for you before the LORD your God. You shall not oppress a hired servant who is poor and needy, whether he is one of your countrymen or one of your aliens who is in your land or in your towns. You shall give him his wages on his day before the sun sets, for he is poor and sets his heart on it; so that he will not cry against you to the LORD and it become sin in you. (Deuteronomy 24:10-15)

Notice the details. First, God tells the one making a loan to remain outside the borrower's house until he gets his pledge—that is, the collateral to secure the loan. Second, if the man to whom the loan is being given is poor, the one making the loan must not keep his collateral (presumably his tunic), but must return it before nightfall. This means, of course, that the one making the loan will effectively be left with no security for the loan. As the passage continues, there is also a requirement that the wages of a hired servant be paid immediately so that he may use the money for his needs. Elsewhere, we find further instructions concerning a poor neighbor:

> Now in case a countryman of yours becomes poor and his means with regard to you falter, then you are to sustain him, like a stranger or a sojourner, that he may live with you. Do not take usurious interest from him, but revere your God, that your countryman may live with you. You shall not give him your silver at interest, nor your food for gain. I am the LORD your God, who brought you out of the land of Egypt to give you the land of Canaan and to be your God. If a countryman of yours becomes so poor with regard to you that he sells himself to you, you shall not subject him to a slave's service. (Leviticus 25:35-39)

Again, notice the details. First, the commands are imperative: *you are to*—not *you may*, or *you should*. Second, while usurious interest may be appropriate in some situations (e.g., Deuteronomy 23:20; Luke 19:23), it was wrong to extract it from a poor person from among Israel's countrymen. He was to be *sustained*—there was no requirement to enrich him. You may *lend* to this poor person, just not at interest. Even if he sold himself to another Israelite (i.e., for indentured service—as was allowed), he was not to be subjected to a slave's service. The people of Israel were not to enrich themselves from a countryman's despair.[3]

---

3. Notice that the obligation was only to help a poor person with basic

It is important to remember that these particular instructions were for the people of Israel and referred to their internal relationships with their own countrymen. However, my sense is that the general principles of love and personally lending a helping hand when a neighbor is down should apply to our conduct as well.

LOVE

Jesus told His followers to emulate God's character, not merely the letter of the law. For example, even though it is not unjust to make a loan with expectation of later repayment, and even under some circumstances to receive interest for it, Jesus said, "Love your enemies, do good to those who hate you, bless those who curse you, pray for those who mistreat you...love your enemies, and do good, and lend, expecting nothing in return; and your reward will be great, and you will be sons of the Most High; for He Himself is kind to ungrateful and evil men. Be merciful, just as your Father is merciful" (Luke 6:27-28, 35-36).

A compelled act is not done from love. When we show love, this is one way we reflect the image of God ("God is love," 1 John 4:8), in which we are made (Genesis 1:26-27). When Jesus was asked what was the greatest commandment, he answered,

> "YOU SHALL LOVE THE LORD YOUR GOD WITH ALL YOUR HEART, AND WITH ALL YOUR SOUL, AND WITH ALL YOUR MIND." This is the great and foremost commandment. The second is like it, "YOU SHALL LOVE YOUR NEIGHBOR AS YOURSELF." On these two commandments depend the whole Law and the Prophets. (Matthew 22:37-40)

---

necessities. There was no moral obligation to lend the poor person interest-free money for an investment in real estate, or business, or some other purpose.

Isaiah 58:6-7, discussed in Chapter 4, presents voluntary sharing with the needy, the hungry, and the homeless as a spiritual directive. The passage continues on to promise that the one who does so will receive his reward from the LORD: "Then your light will break out like the dawn, and your recovery will speedily spring forth; and your righteousness will go before you; the glory of the LORD will be your rear guard" (Isaiah 58:8).

Love is one mark of a person who follows Jesus (John 13:35; 1 John 2:5). James pointed out that love is more than a sentiment; the world only sees it by our actions:

> If a brother or sister is without clothing or in need of daily food, and one of you says to them, "Go in peace, be warmed and filled," and yet you do not give them what is necessary for their body, what use is that? Even so faith, if it has no works, is dead. (James 2:15-17)

DOESN'T LOVE MEAN WE SHOULD ACCEPT SOCIALISM?

"Wait," someone might say, "If Jesus really said to give freely to strangers in need, expecting nothing in return, how can any of His followers object to socialism? Why would any Christian not be willing to pay into a system designed to take care of the most needy people?"

To answer these questions, consider what John could have said, but did not: "If you see a man who has two tunics and another who has none, go and seize one tunic from the man who has two and give it to the man who has none." He did not say that! Nor did he say, "If you see a man who has twenty tunics and another man who has only three, go and seize ten from the man who has twenty, and give seven to the man who has only three, keeping three tunics for yourself and your fellow government bureaucrats."

John's example concerned a man with two tunics, and

a second with *none*, meaning he was naked and in a truly desperate situation. John's concern was not about mathematical equality across all of society, but true need in an individual situation. When you or I encounter a person who is exposed to shame, to the elements, and to the risk of starvation, we must personally help such a person if possible. How far should such kindness extend? "If your enemy is hungry, give him food to eat; and if he is thirsty, give him water to drink" (Proverbs 25:21; cf. Romans 12:20). In other words, even your enemy should have your personal help when in need of life-sustaining assistance.

Remember from Chapter 2 that justice is owed to everyone. A core problem with socialism is that it seeks to address a situation through compulsion and the agency of government that the Bible says ought to be addressed voluntarily by the individual, in love.

SOCIALISM USES THE POOR

Imagine a world in which government taxes some people to support others of lower income. An entire structure, with multiple agencies, hundreds of thousands of employees, contractors, and vendors, becomes established to "help." Billions of dollars flow through this system every year. Politicians get elected and re-elected upon their support for this system, its ongoing funding, and its perpetual growth. Now think about those whose problems are the reason, the *justification*, for all this structure and activity. Do you suppose the system will work to get such people get back onto their own two feet? Think again.

My cousin-in-law, "Nathan,"[4] took a job working for social services in the state of Florida. A young go-getter, and a Christian man with a big heart for people, he was

---

4. I have changed the name since my relative is concerned about retribution.

assigned a case load of 225 families in the Tampa area. He set about his work with genuine zeal; he really wanted to help break the cycle of long-term dependence.

Nathan guided young people through the process of preparing a résumé, taught them how to handle a job interview and dress appropriately for it. He got local banks onboard. He set up job fairs. He ran after-school activities, tutoring, and workshops focused on life skills, soft skills, employability, computer skills, financial literacy, and college prep. And the results began to pour in. Lots of people moved out of government housing, got bank accounts, got their first car, got jobs, or went to college. Ex-felons were getting back into the workforce. One young man became valedictorian and earned a $70,000 college scholarship. Seeing that, a bunch of other kids began really applying themselves in school. Violence in the community dropped dramatically—people were too busy to get in trouble! Law enforcement became more positive.

By the end, Nathan helped an estimated 135-140 people get off government assistance as they took their first steps toward a lifetime of freedom and opportunity.

It had been an uphill battle. The socialist housing assistance programs which he administered included three housing types: income-based, low-income, and zero-income. All three contained strong incentives to keep families broken and dysfunctional, making it more likely that children would be deprived of the well-documented advantages of a two-parent household—and more likely that they would therefore remain trapped in the system as adults. Program rules placed the utmost importance upon *keeping the man out of the house*. His agency had to make sure that the occupants were not receiving any help from the baby's father, and that they were not giving any help to the baby's father. The father of the children couldn't stay at the residence, couldn't have mail sent there, and couldn't be listed on the address.

The system was also designed to disincentivize employment. If someone in the household got a job, the agency would *immediately* reduce the cash assistance being given according to the amount that was now being earned. So, members of the household were left with two choices—either knock yourself out with all the headaches of working many hours, or just do whatever you want with the day and still get the same amount of money. What was even the point of working? The better you do, the more you get penalized. As designed, the system made it seem like only a fool would choose to work. Nathan really had to put a lot of effort into mentoring and motivating these young people, persuading them that it would really be worth it in the long run to break out of the system. But it wasn't easy at all.

The number of federal dollars received by this agency was based upon how many families they had in low-income housing. Nathan's supervisors wanted a jam-packed wait list for housing. As long as they had that wait list, the supervisors were happy. Every month, they would turn in reports detailing employment, education, community service, extracurricular activities, and so forth. If someone went to work, became employed for the first time, went back to school, or got a GED, they would put together a report. Initially, these successes brought more government money, and so his supervisors were happy, but then people started getting jobs and moving out of assisted housing, and they got mad. He was pulled aside and told, "You are young and you want to make a difference. But you will learn over time that there's a lot of money to be made off poor people. So, cool it."

When the local television station got wind of what was happening in the community, Nathan's directors wanted to be the ones interviewed, but the news staff only wanted to talk to him. However, even they came to understand the political implications of the story; they told him so plainly and left out most of the details when the story aired.

You might think that his performance was a success story—and it was! But that is not how his supervisor saw things. She called him into her office, and acknowledged his good work, but then her face turned stern and she said, "You have a for-profit mentality working for a non-profit organization. If you don't stop, you are going to work yourself out of a job." He was stunned.

He started his own "Adopt-a-family" program to help kids and their parents. Around this time, someone even told him he was a threat to national security! The woman who previously headed the neighborhood council told him, "We need bottom feeders." She continued, "If you prove that this can be done, then the trickle-down economics will stop because this is going to spread all over the country."

Nathan's supervisors began requesting anything he did to be filtered through them—they wanted to be copied on all his communications. When one grant ended and a new one began, they somehow kept him on in the same position, and kept paying him, although they did not include him on the new grant. He saw himself being passed over for advancement, and faced what he perceived to be increasing hostility from his superiors. Until then, he had believed the system was in place to help poor people. Now, he learned that it was there to keep them trapped forever, endlessly amassing money and power for those running the system. Harassed and saddened, he soon gave his notice and pursued other work.

Because socialism justifies itself through the existence of people in constant need of government help, socialists inevitably build government structures that penalize self-reliance and throw up barriers that keep people from escaping. Socialists also very often take up programs and initiatives that result in the creation of new "customers" for their services. The recent push to carry out irreversible transgender surgeries on minors—procedures that will set up these precious young people, with their entire lives ahead of them, to require expensive medical care and government assistance for many years to come—is one of many examples of how socialists build their kingdom upon the bodies of the weak and vulnerable.

Notice that a system of taxing the rich to provide for the poor could have existed in ancient Israel; God might easily have commanded it through His prophets. If such an arrangement were just, He surely *would* have commanded it. But He did not. Rather, He told people what their individual stance should be toward the poor. He informed them of their *personal* duty to love their fellow man by sharing their own bread and clothing directly with those in desperate need. And, there is such deep wisdom in this way of helping as opposed to "democratic socialism." Notice that when you or I voluntarily reach into our pockets to help a neighbor in need, we do not have any reason to perpetuate that neighbor's troubles. Rather, we have an opposite incentive—we want to see that neighbor get back to a more stable situation as soon as possible.

CHAPTER SUMMARY

John the Baptist said that the one who has two tunics should share one with the person who has none. A person without even the most basic item of clothing to wear is in desperate need—and is also exposed to public shame. Choosing to help a person we encounter who is in desperate need or immediate danger, when we have the means to do so, is part of our obligation to God, Who made you and me and provides for us daily. Heeding John's exhortation does not require us to approve of socialism, nor would socialism even qualify as a fulfillment of John's instruction.

CHAPTER 11

The Edges of the Field

So far in this book, we've seen many moral provisions for people in need. We've been reminded that God requires us to do justice and also to love mercy. We've reviewed examples of wealthy people like Job who were good stewards of their material possessions. We've seen Christian believers in the book of Acts, for a period of time, voluntarily holding everything in common for the sake of the ministry and in care for each other. We've learned that John the Baptist urged those of his hearers who had an extra garment to share one with him who has none.

As usual, God's ways—which in all of these cases place the moral burden upon the individual—are better and wiser than those recommended by many human advisors. In this chapter, we turn our attention to a special set of instructions God gave to Israel as yet another way of smoothing the road for poor people to get by and get back on their feet. Among God's commandments to Israel as they were about to enter the Promised Land after God delivered them out of slavery in Egypt, there is one that laid responsibility upon private landowners:

Now when you reap the harvest of your land, you shall not reap to the very corners of your field, nor shall you gather the gleanings of your harvest. Nor shall you glean your vineyard, nor shall you gather the fallen fruit of your vineyard; you shall leave them for the needy and for the stranger. I am the LORD your God. (Leviticus 19:9-10; cf. 23:22)

Of the land He was giving them to own and cultivate, God told His people not to gather the gleanings—the last bits or bunches of fruit, missed on the first round of harvest, or the fruit that had fallen to the ground—and to leave the edges of their fields unharvested.[1] In a related command, God told the people of Israel to leave their cultivated land fallow every seventh year, "so that the needy of your people may eat; and whatever they leave the beast of the field may eat. You are to do the same with your vineyard and your olive grove" (Exodus 23:11). These fruits were to be left for the needy and the stranger, and then to the beasts of the field, who could then come and gather what they needed.

What might leaving the edges of the field unharvested look like today? Maybe it would just mean that, if you are a farmer, you should leave the edges uncut for those who may be in need. But I sense that there is a principle which can extend beyond farming. In order to see the principle, let's observe the nature of what is going on in this situation. First, we are talking about a cultivated field—a field which has presumably been plowed and planted by the landowner. In other words, the owner has added his or her own labor and resources into whatever fruit the land is now bearing.

---

1. Rabbis reasoned that the amount to be left should be a sixtieth of the total produce of a field or vineyard. Matthew Henry, *Matthew Henry's Commentary On the Whole Bible*, (Hendrickson Publishers, 1991). I. 407.

However, note that the landowner is not expected to harvest or deliver the produce; it is left up to the needy individual to come and gather. Consider the wisdom of this arrangement: A person in real need will not starve, since he or she will be able to go anywhere in the land during harvest-time and gather fruit or grain. Yet, the system includes a little bit of social discomfort, since neighbors will be able to see who the poor are—and while society will have compassion upon those, such as Ruth and Naomi, who have fallen upon hard unforeseen circumstances, it will be humbling for an able-bodied person to seek sustenance in this way for any extended period. Thus, the system will discourage laziness.

Finally, the produce does not pass through the hands of any ruler or government official. It is left to the one in need to go out personally and expend the energy to gather —and to the landowner, personally, to leave the produce in the fields and allow the gleaners to gather it. Thus, societal relationships are strengthened as everyone does his or her part.

LOVINGKINDNESS, NOT CONDESCENSION

A detail of the command to leave the edges of the field unharvested that stands out to me is the participatory nature of the help extended. God does not treat us as though we are a product or commodity, nor does He ask us to act as though our neighbors are children needing to be waited upon day and night or doted upon as royalty. We all are people of value, made in God's image, who need help, but who also deserve to be treated as individuals.

By loving our neighbor, we honor his Maker. Although we do not look down upon our neighbors as children, we are together children of God, and when anyone is kind to a child, he brings joy to the parent who loves the child.

What does loving others as we love ourselves look like when it comes to the basic needs of life? Remember from the Ten Commandments that we owe it to others not to covet, steal, murder, commit adultery, or steal their good name through false witness, and we owe our parents honor. In the following chapter, we will discuss the parable of the good Samaritan, who went out of his way to show overflowing kindness to a stranger in need. Most of the commandments don't involve *doing* something, but rather, *restraining oneself from action that would harm another*. In the case of the edges of the field, we have a blend of action (planting and cultivating), and restraint (leaving a part unharvested, and not hindering those who gather).

The focus of this book is, of course, discerning what the Bible says about what is right in public policies that purport to meet the material needs of poor people. In the background, we should always remember that God's concern, above all our material needs, is for our eternal safety. Remember that Jesus asked, "What will it profit a man if he gains the whole world and forfeits his soul? Or what will a man give in exchange for his soul?" (Matthew 16:26; cf. Mark 8:36 and Luke 9:25). The eternal consequences of sin, unatoned for, are grave—this life and its concerns are but a breath in light of eternity. I encourage you again to make sure your sins are forgiven (see Chapter 3), and to talk about these things with your children, your friends, and your loved ones (Deuteronomy 11:19).

Finally, as we seek good public policy related to those in need, let's craft our laws in such a way as not to wrong anyone, while also not failing to remember that God is their Provider, just as He is yours. "He executes justice for the orphan and the widow, and shows His love for the alien by giving him food and clothing" (Deuteronomy 10:18).

CHAPTER SUMMARY

As God was taking Israel toward the Promised Land, He gave them the Ten Commandments and various derivative commandments. God's instruction that landowners should leave the edges of their fields unharvested so that the needy and the stranger might gather sustenance provided a way for landowners to love God and their neighbors that did not require breaking any of the other commandments—such as those forbidding theft and coveting. God's commandment did not make landowners harvest the grain or prepare food for the poor —although they certainly could do so if they wished. Rather, the needy would take the initiative and gather what they needed; the landowner was only told to leave it for them.

CHAPTER 12

You Shall Not Oppress A Stranger

"YOU SHALL LOVE THE LORD YOUR GOD WITH
ALL YOUR HEART, AND WITH ALL YOUR SOUL,
AND WITH ALL YOUR STRENGTH, AND WITH ALL
YOUR MIND; AND YOUR NEIGHBOR AS YOUR-
SELF." (Luke 10:27)

Every one of us is supposed to love our neighbors. This imperative is not just for Jews or even only for Christians; although the commandment was given to Israel (Deuteronomy 6 and Leviticus 19:18), Jesus said again and again, "He who has ears to hear, let him hear" (Matthew 11:15; Mark 4:23 and 7:16; Luke 8:8 and 14:35), and as Paul announced in Acts 13:47 (quoting Isaiah 42:6), "I HAVE PLACED YOU AS A LIGHT FOR THE GENTILES, THAT YOU MAY BRING SALVATION TO THE END OF THE EARTH." God, Who made everything, is speaking to everyone He made. That includes you, it includes your neighbors, and it includes people on the other side of the world and across the centuries whom you will never meet.

A lawyer asked Jesus, "And who is my neighbor?" Jesus answered:

> "'A man was going down from Jerusalem to Jericho, and fell among robbers, and they stripped him and beat him, and went away leaving him half dead. And by chance a priest was going down on that road, and when he saw him, he passed by on the other side. Likewise a Levite also, when he came to the place and saw him, passed by on the other side. But a Samaritan, who was on a journey, came upon him; and when he saw him, he felt compassion, and came to him and bandaged up his wounds, pouring oil and wine on them; and he put him on his own beast, and brought him to an inn and took care of him. On the next day he took out two denarii and gave them to the innkeeper and said, "Take care of him; and whatever more you spend, when I return I will repay you." Which of these three do you think proved to be a neighbor to the man who fell into the robbers' hands?' And he said, 'The one who showed mercy toward him.' Then Jesus said to him, 'Go and do the same.'" (Luke 10:30-37)

People who have read the Bible or attended a Bible-teaching church for a long time will find this passage very familiar. Jesus set the story in Israel. The traveler who was attacked and beaten is presumed to be Jewish, and the first two people who passed by were Jewish religious leaders—his own countrymen and the most obvious "neighbors" who should have helped him. The third man, the one who actually *did* help him, was a Samaritan—a man from a neighboring territory whose people hated the Jews and for whom the feeling was mutual. Yet, it was this man, and not the religious countrymen, who helped the victim. And, the kind act of that man was Jesus' answer to the lawyer's question, "And who is my neighbor?"

The story demonstrates, among other things, that the

most distant human being—whether in genetics or culture or homeland—is still our neighbor if we meet him. And since every human bears God's image, the moral obligation to help someone whose life is in immediate danger—as was the case for the man who was beaten to within an inch of death and left on the side of the road—does not end with our own countrymen. When you meet someone in that kind of need, you have an individual moral duty.

On another occasion, Jesus gave a glimpse of the future judgment of those who do not care for the stranger:

> When the Son of Man comes in His glory, and all the angels with Him, He will sit on His glorious throne. All the nations will be gathered before Him, and He will separate the people one from another as a shepherd separates the sheep from the goats. He will put the sheep on His right and the goats on His left. Then the King will say to those on His right, 'Come, you who are blessed by My Father; take your inheritance, the kingdom prepared for you since the creation of the world. For I was hungry and you gave Me something to eat, I was thirsty and you gave Me something to drink, I was a stranger and you invited Me in, I needed clothes and you clothed Me, I was sick and you looked after Me, I was in prison and you came to visit Me.' Then the righteous will answer Him, 'Lord, when did we see You hungry and feed You, or thirsty and give You something to drink? When did we see You a stranger and invite You in, or needing clothes and clothe You? When did we see You sick or in prison and go to visit You?' The King will reply, 'Truly I tell you, whatever you did for one of the least of these brothers and sisters of Mine, you did for Me.' Then He will say to those on His left, 'Depart from Me, you who are cursed, into the eternal fire prepared for the devil and his angels. For I was hungry and you gave Me nothing to eat, I was thirsty

and you gave Me nothing to drink, I was a stranger and you did not invite Me in, I needed clothes and you did not clothe Me, I was sick and in prison and you did not look after Me.' They also will answer, 'Lord, when did we see You hungry or thirsty or a stranger or needing clothes or sick or in prison, and did not help You?' He will reply, 'Truly I tell you, whatever you did not do for one of the least of these, you did not do for Me.' Then they will go away to eternal punishment, but the righteous to eternal life. (Matthew 25:31-46)

It would be wrong to conclude that salvation rests upon our works—it does not ("By the works of the Law no flesh will be justified in His sight," Romans 3:20). But notice the emphasis on individual responsibility. The one who should clothe the naked, invite the stranger in, visit the prisoner, feed the hungry, and give drink to the thirsty is not the government. It is you and me.

IS SOCIALISM NEIGHBORLY?

These passages, then, both emphasize individual moral responsibility. The Good Samaritan did what was right. But is there *anything* in either of these passages to recommend a socialist system of healthcare, housing, or social services? The answer is no. The Good Samaritan's right action was that *he* stopped to avert immediate danger, *he* helped the victim, *he* reached into his *own* pocket, and *he* took time out from whatever he was doing to see that his neighbor—who according to ethnicity and local custom should have been of no account to him—was cared for. Even at the inn, he did not demand anyone else bear the expense, but promised to return and cover the costs himself.

Jesus was answering a question, and it was not, "Who is better, Team Israel or Team Samaria?" Jesus was a Jew

—as were all His disciples—and he loved the Jewish people. But he was teaching how they ought to think about the world, and particularly about the full meaning of God's commandment to "love your neighbor as yourself," shown at the beginning of this chapter. Does "loving your neighbor" mean excusing lawlessness or immoral action? Some people (in my view) misconstrue God's command not to oppress a stranger to mean that an alien must be excused from the consequences of wrongdoing. The Bible, however, is clear that everyone should be subject to the governing authorities (Romans 13:1), so we must conclude that the command not to oppress a stranger does not require us to treat a stranger as though he is above the law.

If you encounter someone at risk of starvation or in medical danger, you should help him—but you have no obligation to facilitate lawlessness. Jesus does not tell people to break laws or engage in theft. Rather, He says, "Go. From now on sin no more" (John 8:11). Some people essentially say the opposite—"Go and sin some more"—and that is wrong.

In Chapter 4, we discussed the poor. The stranger or the alien, being similarly in a position more liable to disadvantage, is mentioned in many of the same verses. Several of these verses tell Israel not to oppress the stranger because they have also been in such a situation. For example, "You shall not oppress a stranger, since you yourselves know the feelings of a stranger, for you also were strangers in the land of Egypt" (Exodus 23:9; cf. 22:21; Deuteronomy 10:18-19). The people of Israel were strangers in Egypt. What went wrong for them? Let's start with Joseph. He was *denied justice*, and wrongly imprisoned for a crime he never committed (Genesis 39:6-20). And later, when a pharaoh arose who did not know Joseph, the people were turned aside from justice and literally enslaved by the Egyptians. That was treating strangers wrongly. Other verses on this topic include Jeremiah 22:3 and Malachi 3:5.

So, we may conclude that not oppressing a stranger includes not wrongly imprisoning him, not enslaving him, not robbing him, and not denying him justice. Many other verses carry on this theme. For example, "The people of the land have practiced oppression and committed robbery, and they have wronged the poor and needy and have oppressed the sojourner without justice" (Ezekiel 22:29; cf. Deuteronomy 24:14; 27:19, "Cursed is he who distorts justice due an alien..."; Leviticus 19:33, "When a stranger resides with you in your land, you shall do him no wrong."). Notice that in all these instances, God is not saying the law must be suspended for the stranger or alien, merely that he must not be wronged.

Equal protection of the laws is accompanied by equal accountability (Leviticus 24:16; cf. 20:2; similar Numbers 15:16 and Leviticus 18:26). The same principle is found elsewhere (for example, Exodus 12:48). God promises blessings to those who maintain such justice and follow God (Jeremiah 7:5-7).

So far, we have spoken of principles—especially justice—that apply both to individuals and to governments. As discussed in Chapter 2, the companion to justice is lovingkindness or mercy, something that is the role of individuals, not governments. For example, "Thus has the LORD of hosts said, 'Dispense true justice and practice kindness and compassion each to his brother; and do not oppress the widow or the orphan, the stranger or the poor; and do not devise evil in your hearts against one another" (Zechariah 7:9-10), and "Do not forget to show hospitality to strangers, for by so doing some people have shown hospitality to angels without knowing it" (Hebrews 13:2), and, "Love does no wrong to a neighbor; therefore love is the fulfillment of *the* law" (Romans 13:10).

Ultimately, we are reminded that God watches over

the strangers (Psalm 146:9; cf. Deuteronomy 10:18-19). A wise man or woman will not pursue harm against those God loves. And, our works should bring glory to God. "Let your light shine before men in such a way that they may see your good works, and glorify your Father who is in heaven" (Matthew 5:16).

CHAPTER SUMMARY

God's concern for the stranger and the alien is similar to His concern for the orphan and the widow. He will watch over them (Psalm 146:9), but He also commands us to not oppress them. The answer to the vulnerable situation for a stranger or alien, however, is not a *double* standard, but an *even* standard, when it comes to justice. And, the individual who has interaction with such a person should show lovingkindness (ḥeṣed) as well.

CHAPTER 13

Honest Weights and Measures

You shall have just balances, just weights, a just ephah, and a just hin; I am the LORD your God, who brought you out from the land of Egypt. (Leviticus 19:36)

Now we come to the most basic principle of justice: honest exchange. We have already seen, in Chapter 9, that fulfilling contractual agreements between parties is right in God's eyes. This principle runs through all economic transactions, and as we shall observe once again in the next few pages, truth is the basis of justice.

BUYING AND SELLING IN THE BIBLE

Wages, or the payment for labor, is a type of purchase. This sort of transaction has already been discussed in Chapters 7, 9, and 12. In essence, wages are not different from buying or selling property; the only distinction is that property is the *residue* of labor, whereas wages are paid for the labor itself, whose fruits are then allocated according to whatever agreement exists between the employer and the one employed.

Beginning in Genesis, there are records of buying and selling. Job certainly acquired his great wealth through just business dealings (Job 1:3). Abraham bought a piece of land on which to bury his wife Sarah (Genesis 23:3-16). Jacob purchased Esau's birthright (Genesis 25:29-34). Following Joseph's counsel, Pharaoh stored up grain during the years of plenty and sold it when the famine struck (Genesis 41:57), using the proceeds to acquire all the land of Egypt (Genesis 47:20-22). Moses offered to purchase food and water if King Sihon would let the Israelites pass through his land (Deuteronomy 2:28). Buying and selling was not to wrong either party (Leviticus 25:14).

As king, David purchased a piece of property on which to erect an altar for burnt offerings to the LORD (2 Samuel 24:24). Boaz negotiated the potential sale of a piece of property on behalf of Naomi (Ruth 4:3). Jeremiah purchased a field from his cousin for an agreed-upon weight of silver, and a deed was signed and sealed before witnesses (Jeremiah 32:9-10). Having to pay for drinking water (an affliction suffered by many city-dwellers even today) and for wood was one sad consequence of Israel's exile to Babylon (Lamentations 5:4).

The chief priests used the thirty pieces of silver given to Judas as payment for betraying Jesus—which he returned before hanging himself—to buy the Potter's Field (Matthew 27:7). On a brighter note, a wise response to the prospect of heaven is likened to that of a man who finds a treasure in a field and then sells all he has in order to buy that field, or to a merchant who sees a pearl of great value and then sells all he has to buy it (Matthew 13:44-46).

Finally, God represents our salvation as a purchase that He paid for in full: "But now, thus says the Lord, your Creator, O Jacob, and He who formed you, O Israel,

'Do not fear, for I have redeemed you" (Isaiah 43:1). His kind offer is stated in Isaiah 1:18, "Though your sins are as scarlet, they will be as white as snow; though they are red like crimson, they will be like wool." The same is referred to in Isaiah 55:1, "Ho! Every one who thirsts, come to the waters; and you who have no money come, buy and eat. Come, buy wine and milk without money and without cost," and, "You were not redeemed with perishable things like silver or gold from your futile way of life inherited from your forefathers, but with precious blood, as of a lamb unblemished and spotless, the blood of Christ" (1 Peter 1:18-19; cf. 1 Corinthians 6:20, 7:23).

These examples of purchase and sale transactions in the Bible show that people from the earliest times operated under a basic understanding of property and its just disposition that generally aligns with what God later made explicit in the Ten Commandments and elsewhere.

GOD HATES LYING SCALES

Like the moral requirement that workers be paid the agreed-upon wages for their labor, justice demands that purchase and sale of goods and property follow the terms agreed, and the terms depend upon a true representation of what is being transacted. If I am told by a seller that I am purchasing a pound of sugar, but he gives me only twelve ounces, I have been cheated. Likewise, if I agree to pay three dollars, but take the item after paying only two, the seller has been cheated. In both cases, one party has been dishonest with the other.

Honest weights and measures in commerce are fundamental to justice throughout the Bible:

> You shall do no wrong in judgment, in measurement of
> weight, or capacity. You shall have just balances, just

weights, a just ephah and a just hin;[1] I am the LORD your God, who brought you out from the land of Egypt. (Leviticus 19:35-36)

Similar statements are found in Deuteronomy 25:13-16, where maintaining justice is linked to a reward of living long in the land which the LORD is giving, and in Proverbs 11:1, "A false balance is an abomination to the LORD, but a just weight is His delight," (similar in 20:10 and 20:23). Proverbs 16:11 states that the weights used in trade are very much God's concern.

Finally, honest standards of measure in human interactions are the image of God's justice in judgment of people. Job asks God to weigh him and his integrity in Job 31:6, and we see a less favorable outcome when God weighs King Belshazzar and finds him wanting in Daniel 5:27. Thieves and swindlers are listed among those who will not inherit the kingdom of God (1 Corinthians 6:10; similar 5:11).

MEANINGLESS WITHOUT PROPERTY

In the late 19th and early 20th century, a con man named George C. Parker repeatedly "sold" the Brooklyn Bridge and other New York landmarks to gullible victims, mostly recent immigrants. Parker posed as the owner and used props such as counterfeit deeds showing ownership and offices set up to make his claims appear truthful. The problem for the victims was that there was nothing behind Parker's claim to own these properties—and therefore he had no right to sell them, and the buyers were accordingly left with nothing to show for the money they paid him.

Fraudsters have existed throughout history. In recent

---

1. The ephah and the hin were units of measure for grain and liquid respectively.

years, internet scams in which a Nigerian "prince" promises great reward for help in transferring his money out of the country, and many variations on this con, have captured innocent victims. The problem in all these instances is that there is no *truth* to the con-man's claims and promises.

If we bring this principle around to God's commands not to steal and not to covet (see Chapter 6), to pay the worker his wages (Deuteronomy 24:15; Jeremiah 22:13; Malachi 3:5; James 5:4), Peter's affirmation that Ananias and Sapphira owned their property (see Chapter 8), and even the command to share with the one in need (see Chapters 10 and 11), we must recognize that none of these commandments and statements would make any sense if there was no *truth* behind people's ownership of their property—that is, their labor and its fruits.

CHAPTER SUMMARY

Justice in human economic relationships rests upon truth. God's love of honest trade, and His burning anger against those who cheat in their trade, is evident throughout the Bible. A buyer should receive the product that is purchased, not less—and a seller should receive the value agreed upon for what he sells. The system rests upon a premise that buyer and seller, employer and employee, *own* their labor and their property. Without such affirmation, honest trade would be without foundation. Since socialism denies any necessary right to property, it cannot be called just.

CHAPTER 14

Jubilee

W e come now to a particular arrangement that
God decreed for His people Israel when they
entered the Promised Land, to consider what,
if any, bearing it might have upon the question before us,
the moral assessment of socialism.

In the sabbath years and the year of Jubilee, detailed
in Leviticus 25, we find a beautiful picture of God's grace.
Let's look at the passage in order to understand it, along
the way giving attention to its rules for property and its
disposition.

> You shall thus consecrate the fiftieth year and proclaim
> a release through the land to all its inhabitants. It shall
> be a jubilee for you, and each of you shall return to his
> own property. You shall have the fiftieth year as a ju-
> bilee; you shall not sow, nor reap its aftergrowth, nor
> gather in from its untrimmed vines. For it is a jubilee; it
> shall be holy to you. You shall eat its crops out of the
> field. On this year of jubilee each of you shall return to
> his own property. If you make a sale, moreover, to your
> friend or buy from your friend's hand, you shall not

wrong one another. Corresponding to the number of years after the jubilee, you shall buy from your friend; he is to sell to you according to the number of years of crops. In proportion to the extent of the years you shall increase its price, and in proportion to the fewness of the years you shall diminish its price, for it is a number of crops he is selling you. So you shall not wrong one another, for you shall fear your God; for I am the LORD your God. (Leviticus 25:10-17)

The Jubilee was a reset, scheduled in advance to occur every fiftieth year, restoring the land to the original owners after it had been "sold" to others during the interim. God was bringing Israel into the land He had promised to them, giving it to them as an *everlasting inheritance*.[1] Israel was not purchasing it; they were conquering it with God's help and blessing after being brought by Him out of Egypt, "by a mighty hand and by an outstretched arm" (Deuteronomy 5:15 and many others), with the very purpose of taking possession of this land. Part of God's plan for Israel involved a division of the land among the twelve tribes. Partly to preserve these ancestral allocations, God ordered this periodic reversion of the land to the family to whom it was first allocated by lot.

Jubilee affirms property, with a caveat. The land was owned by those to whom it was first assigned. But can a man really be said to own that which he is not at liberty to alienate—that is, to sell? In fact, we do have examples of such ownership even today. When an airline, a sports franchise, or a concert venue sells tickets, the seller often designates the ticket as "non-transferable," meaning that the original purchaser has a right to use the ticket, but

---

1. "I will give to you and to your descendants after you, the land of your sojournings, all the land of Canaan, for an everlasting possession; and I will be their God" (Genesis 17:8).

acquires no right to sell or gift it to another person. The non-transferability would generally be upheld by law because that limitation was part of the original contract under which the ticket was sold.

God intended the Promised Land to be Israel's everlasting inheritance. For this purpose to be made effective and durable, the land needed to be inalienable from the families to whom it was first allocated. This end is, I believe, the underlying purpose of the law of Jubilee. And, it does not undermine the principle of private property, because, after all, the owners to whom the land was allocated did retain a right to the land, to its use, and to its increase. The fruits and other increase of the land was the possession of those who owned it or—as we also notice— who purchased it for a period of time until the arrival of the next Jubilee year.

So, let's review and summarize. First, the *land* is restored to the original owner, but not the wealth generated thereby during the time it was used by those who purchased it. Second, God's instructions included the repeated command to not wrong one another. The land was to be "sold" for only the remaining number of years until Jubilee. Since these details would be known at the time of purchase, the buyer would know he was acquiring only temporary use of the land—that is, the crops the land would bring forth during that time period. And finally, God's design states that the seller is the buyer's *friend*. While buyer and seller are naturally both seeking to maximize their own interests and profits, they are also working together, each one giving the other something of value: The buyer gives the seller an agreed amount of money or a portion of the crops, and the seller gives the buyer the land to use for the time period agreed.

REST FOR THE LAND, DEBTS FORGIVEN, SLAVES SET FREE

But there is more to the year of Jubilee than mere return of land. If anyone owed a debt to another person, that debt had to be forgiven with the sounding of the trumpet on the Day of Atonement. If anyone was bound to service, he or she would go free at that moment.[2] The Jubilee was to be a year of liberty, a year of restoring people and making them whole, of lifting the heavy weight of debt, shame, and servitude off their shoulders.

JUBILEE POINTED TO JESUS

We do not know how consistently the Jubilee was enforced throughout Israel, but its theological weight is immense either way. The tenth day of the seventh month, when the ram's horn was to be sounded and Jubilee was to begin, was Yom Kippur, the Day of Atonement.

More than a thousand years later, when Jesus was handed the scroll in the synagogue, as recounted in Luke 4:16-21, He found and read the passage referring to Jubilee and the One anointed (Messiah) to proclaim it: "The Spirit of the Lord God is upon me, because the LORD has anointed me to bring good news to the afflicted; He has sent me to bind up the brokenhearted, to proclaim liberty to captives and freedom to prisoners; to proclaim the favorable year of the Lord" (Isaiah 61:1-2). Then, He gave it back to the attendant and said to those

---

2. People sometimes sold themselves or even their family into service to satisfy a debt that they had no other way of paying. The slavery referenced might also have included enslaved captives from war. Slavery will be discussed in the next chapter, but the system of slavery talked about in the Bible talks about is not the same as the chattel slavery that prevailed in the American south and other parts of the world until the 19th century.

present, "Today this Scripture has been fulfilled in your hearing."

Jesus thus identified Himself as the Messiah, and associated His work with the Jubilee—when debts are canceled, slaves are freed, and those God rescues return to the inheritance He gave them. There is much more to be said on this subject. The fact that no work was to be done on the Jubilee was also important, in light of the fact that it extended the Day of Atonement—when atonement is made *for you* (Leviticus 16:30)—and that Jesus said, "Come to Me, all who are weary and heavy-laden, and I will give you rest" (Matthew 11:28). Jesus' second coming will be announced in a similar fashion, yet another reason theologians acknowledge that the Jubilee foreshadows Him (1 Thessalonians 4:16; cf. 1 Corinthians 15:52).

CHAPTER SUMMARY

The year of Jubilee was a special arrangement for Israel in the Promised Land that preserved the allocation of territories among the twelve tribes of Israel. The owners had no right to permanently sell their land to others, only to lease it for the remaining number of years until the next Jubilee, at which time all slaves or indentured servants were also to be set free, and all debts completely canceled. Since the Jubilee could always be foreseen, people could plan accordingly. Thus, Jubilee is not inharmonious with the Bible's moral affirmation of property. Finally, the deep meaning of the clean slate was at the same time freeing to those who would otherwise be without hope, and also a poignant and powerful shadow of Jesus' then-yet-to-come atoning work.

CHAPTER 15
Slavery

An involuntary slave is someone forced to work for another against his or her will, or whose labor and its fruit is taken by others without the laborer's consent. There are some circumstances when law and custom justly permit such compulsion and do not call it slavery. For example, no one but the grumbling child calls the parent who makes him wash the dishes before going out to play a "slavedriver," and many jurisdictions also permit those duly convicted of crimes to work without compensation as part of punishment and restitution to society. But generally, forced servitude is slavery.

So-called "democratic socialism" is the enslavement of taxpayers. Under it, the slaveholders are those to whom resources or property are redistributed, and the slave traders are the socialist politicians who chose to do the slaveholders' dirty work.

Mark parks his car, a beautiful and well-maintained Porsche Carrera, by the curb. Mark, a widower, is 64 years old. A carpenter since high school, he has been a hard worker and a careful steward of money his entire life. Following the death of his wife Nancy from cancer several years ago, he downsized. His single luxury is this car, paid off only last month.

"Nice wheels," says John, appearing from nowhere.

"Yeah," agrees John's girlfriend Kira, standing nearby.

"I don't have a car like that," says John. "Let's take a vote on whether we can take that sweet ride off your hands."

"Uh, no thanks," says Mark, backing away.

John grips him firmly on the shoulder. "I'll take that as your vote is 'no,' old man. Babe, what's yours?"

"Oh yeah, yes—absolutely," says Kira, eyeing the car.

"Well, how about that," says John, "My vote's 'yes' too. The people have spoken! Now—hand over the keys." John's firm grip is matched by an icy gaze, his nose just an inch from Mark's. A blade flashes in his left hand, suddenly pressed in just below Mark's ribcage. Mark raises the keys and drops them into Kira's open palm.

A vote was taken, and two-thirds of the voters agreed that Mark's property should be redistributed to John and Kira. So, what is the big problem? According to so-called "democratic socialists," justice was done!

But, it was not. That car was Mark's property. It was his because he purchased it with his own money, the residue of his labor. And even if his money had been gifted to him or inherited or gained by thoughtful investments, it was still the fruit of labor. By stealing it from him, Kira and John forced Mark into slavery, seizing his labor without his consent—since he voted "no."

Under democratic socialism, people who covet the property of others use the democratic process and the agencies of government to steal what they want. Elections give a veneer of respectability to the transaction, but the process does not alter its true nature. Wealth redistribution against the will of the one from whom it is taken is involuntary servitude, otherwise known as slavery.

SERVITUDE AND JUSTICE

Slavery has taken different forms over the centuries and even today. The most important piece of information when making a moral judgment about slavery concerns whether the arrangement is compelled or voluntary. My purpose in this book is to present what the Bible says, not to impose my own preference. We are not wiser than God. We, rather, should seek understanding, with care and humility.

The chattel slavery commonly practiced in many parts of the world until the late 19th and even early 20th centuries was fueled by the capture of unwilling victims, their transport under cruel and filthy conditions for sale in a foreign land, and the subsequent multi-generational bondage of those captured and their descendants. It was a crushing and evil trade.

Although the Bible does in various places acknowledge and even accept the existence of slavery in one form or another,[1] we must not jump to general conclusions and should not assume that the slavery mentioned in the Bible is everywhere equal to that with which we are familiar from recent world history. Remember what we have already established in Chapter 2 concerning God's love of

---

1. In Deuteronomy 20:11, God told Israel that all the people found in a city that agreed to peace after Israel approached to fight against it would become forced labor and serve Israel. Elsewhere (Joshua 16:10, 17:13; Judges 1:30, 33, 35) we learn that some Canaanites who were not driven out completely became forced labor to Israel. Solomon forced at least 30,000 people of Israel into labor, rotating one month on and two months off, to build the temple and other structures (1 Kings 4:6, 5:13-14, 9:15, 21). God's sanction of Solomon's use of forced labor in these projects is not explicit. But it is probably worth observing that these were national projects for the people who were conscripted—people were not enslaving others for personal service.

116

justice. God would not command people to do injustice, and He would never command people to sin in any other way: "Let no one say when he is tempted, 'I am being tempted by God'; for God cannot be tempted by evil, and He Himself does not tempt anyone" (James 1:13). So, we know that God does not lead people into evil.

Proceeding upon the understanding that God does not lead anyone into evil, we turn now to Exodus 21:2-11 and immediately see that it is a difficult passage, because in it God appears to condone activities that seem unjust according to other parts of the Bible. It gives rules for buying, keeping, and freeing Hebrew slaves. It confirms that the children of enslaved persons belong to the master. It confirms that a man may sell his daughter as a female slave (presumably for conjugal purposes). And it confirms certain rights that such a woman shall have that are similar to the rights a wife has over her husband. The passage provides that a Hebrew male slave must go free without any requirement of payment after six years of service, yet denies such freedom to a daughter sold as a female slave.

Before offering comment on the Exodus 21 passage, please read the following so that we may consider the matter in light of both passages.

> As for your male and female slaves whom you may have —you may acquire male and female slaves from the pagan nations that are around you. Then, too, it is out of the sons of the sojourners who live as aliens among you that you may gain acquisition, and out of their families who are with you, whom they will have produced in your land; they also may become your possession. You may even bequeath them to your sons after you, to receive as a possession; you can use them as permanent slaves. But in respect to your countrymen, the sons of Israel, you shall not rule with severity over one another. (Leviticus 25:44-46)

DANIEL ALAN BRUBAKER

A basic principle of biblical interpretation is that Bible passages open to several possible meanings should generally be understood so as to harmonize with others on the same topic that are open to only one possible meaning.

Servitude can be either voluntary or involuntary. Let's consider what, historically, has led to each. Someone in involuntary servitude may have been taken captive through kidnapping or might be a captive of war, either sold by the victors or kept as a slave. He might have been born to someone already in servitude, in a society that provides for children to follow the condition of an enslaved parent. And finally, hard as it is for me as a father to imagine, a child may have been sold into servitude by the parent—for example, to satisfy a debt.

By contrast, a person under voluntary servitude often sold himself into service for a specified number of months or years, or a certain number of hours per day. Regular employment is one type of voluntary servitude: Someone agrees to labor for a period of time in exchange for something valuable, usually money. A person who freely sells himself into servitude has basically entered a contract. Also in this category we find people in servitude as a consequence of lawful prosecution for some crime.

Are all forms of involuntary servitude unjust? Are the passages shown above prescriptive (i.e., do they say what *should* be done) or merely descriptive (i.e., do they merely state what *was* done)? I do not know what to make of the Exodus 21 passage. In light of the other commandments, it is reasonable to conclude that Deuteronomy 20:11 was a specific command only to Israel in that time. As should be evident from the earlier parts of this book, particularly Chapters 6 through 8, involuntary servitude is wrong except in limited circumstances such as a person convicted of a crime or for a national building project. The worker is worthy of his wages (1 Timothy 5:18), and the principle of property affirms ownership unless and until the worker willingly parts with his labor or its fruits. Jesus said, "In everything, therefore, treat people the same way you want them to treat you, for this is the Law and the Prophets" (Matthew 7:12). Would you want to be sold into slavery against your will? Or held in slavery? If not, then do not do it to someone else.

"That's not the same thing," someone may say, "It is insulting and offensive to compare socialism, which *helps* people, with slavery, which everyone knows was a disgrace, a stain upon the world!" However, being offended is not an answer. We've established that everyone, rich and poor alike, is owed justice. It is wrong to enslave some people in the name of helping others. Does Mark deserve to be enslaved just because he'd saved enough money to buy a Porsche? Remember, some souls kidnapped into slavery from Africa and elsewhere were from noble and wealthy families. Does that mean in your mind that such people somehow deserved to be enslaved? If not, then Mark did not deserve it either.

Stealing Mark's car was not as bad as the lifetime of bondage endured by the slaves of the 17th-19th centuries. However, the nature of the injustice is the key question, not the degree. What if Mark was not just a humble carpenter of average means, but rather an extremely wealthy man with multiple cars, several homes, a yacht, and a private jet? What would be the harm, in that case, of forcing him to give some of his wealth to others less fortunate than he? The question remains, "Is it involuntary servitude?" The answer, I suggest, can be nothing but "Yes." Furthermore, the commandments "You shall not steal," and "You shall not covet" (Exodus 20:15, 17) still apply. The use of a third party—in this case, the government—to carry out the plunder does not change the nature of the activity.

CHAPTER SUMMARY

Democratic socialism is a system of involuntary servitude, in which a minority population is forced to labor for the majority. This slavery goes by various euphemisms that include "welfare," "affordable housing," "student loan forgiveness," and so on. Because the government cannot be resisted, the enslaved have no choice but to serve as commanded. Even if they decide to flee, in virtually no instance can they do so without first having their labor—in the form of whatever portion of their wealth is demanded—seized by the will of the majority. Since the Bible affirms that labor and its fruits belong to the individual to dispose of as he wishes, democratic socialism is incompatible with biblical justice.

CHAPTER 16

My Brother's Keeper?

Have you ever heard Christians or others use the term "brother's keeper" as though it is somehow a good or desirable thing, as though it is something we all should want to be?

The *only* place the words "brother's keeper" occur in the entire Bible are in the mouth of the murderous Cain.

> And it came about when they were in the field, that Cain rose up against Abel his brother and killed him. Then the LORD said to Cain, "Where is your brother?" And he said, "I do not know. Am I my brother's keeper?" He said, "What have you done? The voice of your brother's blood is crying to Me from the ground." (Genesis 4:8-10)

Did God tell Cain to be his brother's keeper? Did God mean for Cain to be his brother's keeper? In fact, nowhere does the Bible imply that Cain was supposed to be a paternalistic figure, infantilizing his brother Abel by providing for his every need or want. No. The justice that Cain owed to his brother Abel was to *not murder him!*

Are you and I meant to provide free healthcare, housing, food, childcare, phones, price controls, rent control, and a "living wage"? If that is your specific calling from God, then yes, on an individual basis you should do those things (not price controls or rent control, of course, because these are theft) that God has called you and enabled you to do. But will God ever call you to snatch a purse from a woman on the street in order to provide housing to someone else? I highly doubt it.

Friends, let us be very careful not to take what is evil and call it good. If you hear a Christian saying that we need to be our "brother's keeper," please rebuke that person. Remind that person that every man, woman, and child is made in God's image and that every person with his faculties about him has agency—given to him by God. This agency includes the ability to make choices in life, to take moral responsibility for his actions, and to interact with other human beings on an equal level, not as a child seeking permission from an older sibling or a parent. Except when it is actually required by old age, young age, or a debilitating health condition, we do not need to be changing each other's diapers or preparing a bottle to place in the mouth of our fellow men and women. No. We owe our fellow human beings *justice*. And we owe them lovingkindness. Paternalism—seeing ourselves as a "brother's keeper" to others—is neither.

DOES YOUR PROPERTY REALLY BELONG TO THE POOR?

Along with the popular misconception that the Bible somehow instructs us to be like hovering mother chickens over our fellow humans, there is a corollary belief that such a paternalistic attitude requires those who have some quantity of property—great or small—to lie down and allow others (members of a category called "the poor") to just take whatever they like.

Several years ago, a Christian friend informed me that my property really "belongs to God and, by extension, to the poor." I did not understand then, nor do I now, how she arrived at the conclusion that if something belongs to God, then it belongs to the poor. But since her line of reasoning in support of socialism is possibly held by others, let us consider it.

This friend asserted that, "capitalism says that your property belongs to you. The Bible says that your property belongs [...] to the poor." I see in this statement two core assertions: First, your property does not belong to you—presumably because it belongs to God, as mentioned above—and second, your property does belong to the poor. Having read this far in the book, I suspect that you can easily see the errors, which we might expose through a series of questions.

First, if the poor own my property, then what could possibly be the meaning of the commandment, "You shall not steal"? Does it apply only to some people and not to others? Do only poor people own things, and do they therefore own everything—that is to say, all of my property, as my friend asserted? In Matthew 19:18, Jesus told a man that he should keep the commandment not to steal. What did Jesus mean? Was Jesus lying to him? Did he mean only that one should not steal from the poor, who own everything, because it would be impossible to steal from those who are not poor, since they own nothing? Was Jesus just presenting this man with some weird riddle?

Second, if it is true that the poor own everything, how is this conclusion reached from the Bible, and—importantly—what is the definition of "poor"? Put differently, perhaps, if I become poor, then will I own everything and have the right to walk into any non-poor person's home and take whatever I like? The answer to such questions would seem very important, also, so that I can know who is allowed to take my car, hack into my bank account, take my house, carry away my books and photographs and personal effects, and who is not allowed to do this (i.e., because they are not "poor," and therefore do not own my property).

Was the thief on the cross next to Jesus actually innocent—at least of theft? Or was he just not poor enough to own everything? In Acts 5, we learn that Peter told Ananias that his land belonged to him—i.e., Ananias—before it was sold, and that after it was sold, the money was at his —i.e., Ananias'—disposal. Was Peter lying to Ananias?

In the Parable of the Workers in the Vineyard (Matthew 20), the moral weight of the story rests upon the truth that the landowner actually owned his land and his money, and therefore had a right to do with it what he wished—in that case, paying the workers different hourly wages as agreed in contracts to which they had individually assented. If the landowner did not own his property, then Jesus would have been likening God to an unjust landowner. Can there be any reason that Jesus would have sought to demonstrate God's justice by explaining that it is very much like human injustice?

Why would God bother giving the commandment "You shall not covet" if everyone's property actually belongs to the poor? It would seem, at least, that He would have qualified it so we would know when coveting exists. That is, if I am not a poor person and I covet another person's house, then it is coveting, but if I am poor, then everyone's house actually belongs to me, so there is no way I could covet even if I tried, unless perhaps I am coveting the property of another poor person?

This conundrum is one of the biggest areas of confusion for me. There are many poor people (at least that is what Tevye says in *Fiddler on the Roof*). When you say that the poor own my property, how is this borne out in reality? Does every poor person in the world own an equal share of my property? Or is any given poor person just entitled to take whatever he likes of my property, which by staking his claim (like the settlers in the Wild West) then becomes "his?" And, if poor people actually own all the property in the world (because the property of everyone who is not "poor" actually belongs to those who are "poor"), what is the meaning of "poor," anyway? Does it actually mean "The only type of person in the world who owns property"?

CHAPTER SUMMARY

Using the term "my brother's keeper" in a positive manner is usually a sign of biblical illiteracy. We owe it to our fellow men to treat them fairly, and doing so includes respecting their property. Ultimately, it is true that everything we have is God's (Psalm 24:1). But, in human relationships, God gave instructions for the orderly disposition of property, made each of us stewards of the property we own, and commanded us to respect the property of others. When we steal, whether by breaking and entering or by voting to take someone's property and give it to another, we thumb our noses at God's word and break the two greatest commandments, to love the LORD your God with all your heart, and to love your neighbor as yourself.

CHAPTER 17

What's Wrong With Socialism

O n August 4, 2016, little Charlie was born in London, England, a country with a socialist healthcare system called the National Health Service (NHS). Though Charlie was apparently healthy when he was born at full term, his parents noticed after a few weeks that he was not gaining weight and exhibited some weakness. Tests eventually revealed a rare genetic disease that would likely lead to death in infancy following brain damage and organ failure. In November of the same year, the hospital ethics board recommended against giving Charlie a tracheostomy, and his condition worsened.

Then, in December, Charlie's parents consulted with Dr. Michio Hirano, Columbia University Medical Center's chief of the Division of Neuromuscular Disorders. In January, a GoFundMe account was begun for Charlie; it raised £1.3 million (roughly $1.5 million) within a few months. The local UK hospital in January opined that some epileptic seizures had likely caused brain damage in Charlie, and the hospital began discussing ending his life support. His parents disagreed and wanted to take him to New York for nucleoside treatment with Dr. Hirano.

Rather than allow the parents, who had raised the funds for the transfer to New York, to take Charlie and go, the local socialist hospital began to *fight his parents in court in order to stop them from taking him*. The courts of Britain supported the hospital's efforts to block Charlie's transfer. It also took a major fight from Charlie's parents and a significant public outcry to stop the hospital's plan to take Charlie off life support on June 30. Even President Donald Trump got involved in the case, as did congressmen Brad Wenstrup and Trent Franks, who offered to introduce a bill to grant Charlie and his family lawful permanent resident status in the U.S., and support the parents in their right to choose what they felt was best for their son, rather than be ordered to let him die by Britain's single-payer healthcare system. By the time appeals had worked through the courts, Charlie was still alive, but when Dr. Hirano visited him in July, he determined that it was now too late for treatment. Life support was withdrawn at the end of July, and Charlie died the next day.

Charlie's story attracted a lot of attention, but it was sadly not an isolated case. In 2020, the COVID-19 virus traversed the world in a pandemic that caused deaths mostly among older people and those with multiple other underlying health conditions. Now, in a pandemic, every country, state, and locality must sometimes contend with supply chain issues as demand for materials outpaces ordinary demands. For times of medical crisis with limited resources and facilities, triage protocols exist. But what happens when people's individual value to those providing health services is based in some way upon a formula involving their perceived future contribution to society versus the cost to "the system" of keeping them alive?

As was reported in mid-2021, the NHS in 2017 and

2018 drafted protocols to withdraw hospital care from nursing home residents in the event of a future pandemic. As confirmed by Whitehall documents, the plans would refuse treatment to nursing home residents in their 70s, instead offering "support" in the form of various "end of life pathways."[1] And, the plan was carried out: NHS managers asked elderly care homes and general practitioners "to place 'do not resuscitate' orders on all residents at the height of the [COVID-19] pandemic to keep hospital beds free."[2] When resources were limited, patients were triaged according to their perceived likelihood of survival instead of their clinical need. As Whitehall documents further confirm, the policy was classified as "confidential" and "official sensitive," and therefore kept from public knowledge and debate.[3]

But *why* would socialist countries favor "end of life pathways" for patients in nursing homes? What could be their incentive for doing such a thing? After all, the glorious utopia of "free" healthcare should be available to everyone in unlimited quantities, right? Again, socialism rests upon a materialist philosophy and a low view of the value of individual humans. Under socialism, government provides services, doing so with money collected in taxes, with higher income individuals typically bearing the brunt of such taxation. But the total quantity of funds available for those services is limited!

Furthermore, allocation of those funds is not driven by ordinary market forces, but rather by political forces, including by individuals who are neither subject matter experts, nor masters in the management of a highly complex business. These political operators are typically not

---

1. "NHS made pandemic plan to deny elderly care," *Daily Telegraph*, 31 July 2021. telegraph.co.uk (December 2, 2024, ProQuest International Newsstream).
2. Ibid.
3. Ibid.

held accountable for failure of the business to run most efficiently within budgetary constraints. That is to say, there is a great deal more waste in a government-run system funded by tax dollars than there would be within a company that has to compete in a free market with quality service at a good price while paying all the employees and contractors a mutually acceptable wage.

Well, someone may object, *that may indeed be bad, but at least people had access to free healthcare. And anyway, isn't a capitalist system much worse at taking care of the poor and needy?* The answer to this question could take various forms and fill volumes, but let's pick just one. Think of the countries that have been socialist for decades, and those that have been capitalist for decades (or more). Which ones are perceived as the greatest destinations by prospective immigrants? While it is true that immigrants have flooded countries like Germany, France, and the UK, and have been immediately signed up for their social services, the leading country for immigration in the world remains the free-market United States. And there are no floods of people clamoring to get into socialist "paradises" like North Korea, or Cuba, or China.

The Berlin Wall was erected by the Soviet Union between East Germany and West Germany. The purpose of the wall was not to keep people out; it was to prevent citizens of the U.S.S.R. from fleeing. You don't have to erect barriers to exit when the governing system is better than what is on the other side of the border. But Communist countries regularly bar people from emigration.

SOCIALISM MISREPRESENTS REALITY

In late 2024, socialist U.S. senator Bernie Sanders wrote, "The top 1% of Americans have taken $50 trillion dollars (sic) from the bottom 90% in the last 50 years. And you wonder why people in this country are angry?"[4] Now, when we are told that somebody "took" something, we do not assume that they bought it, or worked for it, or were given it. But Sanders' accusation—in addition to being incredibly misleading because of social mobility factors to be discussed below—was disingenuous. In a linked video of his own speech, Sanders did not say "taken," but rather "transfer of wealth," also misleading.

Statistics, when abused, distort the world they purport to depict. Much of the discussion in western countries around poverty—especially in the United States—distorts critical detail, or omits it altogether. The economist Thomas Sowell has pointed out that household income, a metric most often cited as evidence of disparity, often hides the real situation, since top earning households have more people living together and average *four times as many income earners* as bottom earning households. Sowell asks, "How surprising is it when four people working earn more income than one person earning?"[5]

Sowell also cited a University of Michigan study that followed a set of working Americans from 1975 to 1991. This study found that 95% of the people who started in the bottom 20 percent of individual earners were no longer in that category by the end—and a stunning 29% actually rose all the way to the top 20% of earners.[6] Only one out of every twenty people in that study remained in poverty after 16 years. This finding highlights an important fact: poverty is often a stage of life, and it is overwhelmingly a *temporary* condition. At least in the United States (where opportunities abound), very few people remain in poverty for a greatly extended period of time.

Cheerleaders for socialism like Bernie Sanders, of

---

4. Bernie Sanders, post on X, December 3, 2024.
5. Thomas Sowell, *Discrimination and Disparities*, (New York: Basic Books, 2019). 90.
6. Ibid., 92.

course, tend to dislike such clarity. Of those 29% who moved from the bottom to the top in the Michigan study, one would be right to wonder how many would have done the same under a socialist system? Also, if 29% who started at the bottom moved all the way to the top category at some point over a period of *sixteen years*, what is likely to have happened to the "bottom 90%" referenced by Bernie Sanders over his period of *fifty years*? The answer is that the categories are not static; his words are essentially lies because of the detail he omits.

SOCIALISM IS INTERNALLY INCONSISTENT

Notice the following features about socialism. Socialism is *optimistic* about human nature corporately when the group being discussed is government, but *pessimistic* about human nature corporately when the group being discussed is involved in any sort of private or for-profit enterprise, and *pessimistic* about the individual at all times except when that individual is acting as a government agent. The individual apart from government is presented as either *helpless and in need of rescue* or as *an oppressor of others*. If you stop just a moment and think about it, socialists' arguments make no sense. What would cause the same person to have the purest possible motives when wearing a government badge, but the most evil and corrupt motives when sitting at the board table of his corporation?

SOCIALISM IS UNKIND

Since regular market forces of supply and demand don't work the same way when there is a monopoly, supplies are less likely to be sufficient in every situation. For this reason, socialism always winds up rationing; it is tragic that some people eager for socialism today don't yet understand, because they have not lived it. When government either owns the means of production, or micromanages them through needling regulations and processes, the invisible hand of the free market is chained up and locked away. The result—as millions have discovered the hard way over the last century—is bread lines, power cuts, empty supermarket shelves, high prices, and rationed or subpar healthcare—all of these accompanied by ever-increasing taxes to counterbalance government waste and inefficiency. Because of its inevitable results, those who push socialism onto society do a very unkind thing.

FORCED "COMPASSION" HARMS US ALL

Think for a moment of a time when you saw or learned of someone in need, someone who had nothing to offer you in return, and you reached into your own pocket and handed that person a gift that actually *cost you* something. How did it make you feel? It felt good, didn't it? Your day had more meaning. You felt more alive. You felt joy. You felt *human*.

You were not, in fact, any more human after this encounter, but the feeling you experienced is one of many reflections of God's image in you. God made you, He is love (1 John 4:8), and something feels right in your life when you choose to love others in a way that costs you something personally.

Now imagine that you are taxed heavily, day after day, month after month, and year after year, to support a government that provides healthcare, housing, free college, and a "universal basic income." Someone approaches you on the street asking for help to buy food or to pay for a temporary lodging. What is your first thought? Whether you say it out loud or not, probably it is, "What do I pay my taxes for? There are all kinds of resources available to you. I've already paid for your housing, your food, your clothing, and probably even your smartphone. Why should I pay for these things *twice* by giving you more?"

And you might refer them to the nearest government assistance office.

How do you feel after that interaction? Likely, you walk away from this encounter feeling at least a bit annoyed—maybe directly toward that person for making you look unkind by saying "no" when he should know that there are government resources available. Or, if he does manage to persuade you to give, you probably feel at least a little resentful toward those who have been bleeding you dry financially and still have not managed to adequately meet the needs of people like the one who approached you for a handout.

Now, think about a time you were in need and had to ask someone else for help. How did it make you feel? Probably embarrassed, even a little ashamed, right? Also, you felt vulnerable and uncertain how your need was going to be met, or if it would be met at all. You had to face the possibility—or maybe even the reality—of missing a meal, or of getting by on very little, or of spending the night in an uncomfortable, unclean, or even possibly unsafe place.

Then, someone gave you some money, or food, or a place to stay. What did you feel then? Perhaps you felt humbled and grateful. Your heart was warmed that a complete stranger cared enough to help you. Your sense of belonging to the human family was renewed, as was that of the one who helped you.

Compelled compassion cultivates callous hearts. We often talk about unintended consequences, but one of the greatest, and gravest, consequences of socialism is a deadening of the human spirit and the fabric of society. The late U.S. Supreme Court justice, Antonin Scalia, once wrote, "The transformation of charity into legal entitlement has produced donors without love and recipients without gratitude." He was right.

Then we come to our need for the satisfaction of reward following effort. Being given everything by government, even possibly feeling entitled to what you did not earn, differs from having to work to provide food for yourself and your family or acquire those other things you may want or need. There are times when each one of us will need to rely upon others—in childhood, in old age, through illness or debilitating disease, during periods of job loss or betrayal by a spouse, and so forth—and it is not wrong to accept help during times of need. But if most of us go through life without experiencing the joy of reward for our effort, we will have missed an important part of what we were made for, what it means to be human and made in the image of God, Who worked six days to create everything (Genesis 2:2), and Who continues to work (John 5:17).

Now, multiply the impact of not experiencing the joy of reward for work—nor the joy of regular voluntary self-sacrifice in care for others—across billions of interactions, over many years, throughout an entire society. What do you suppose will be the cumulative effect on the general health and condition of the soul of that place? It will be negative when compared to the outcome when it is left to individuals to see needs and meet them.

There is a reason that socialist and communist societies lack overflowing joy. I even notice it in post-communist countries that have yet to fully recover from the oppression. Smiles are often hollow. And in the eyes of so many there is an emptiness, a pessimism, a lack of joy. I believe that the reason is similar to that which makes plants grown under fluorescent lights or in poor soil look wilted and sickly. Masses of people under socialism are systemically denied key nutrients that their souls really need in order to flourish.

THE DREADFUL CONSEQUENCES OF SYSTEMIC INJUSTICE

The common good is a term loved by socialists. The term appears exactly once in the Bible—1 Corinthians 12:7—and the verse refers neither to economics nor coercion.[7] The problem with using the term "common good" in economic discussions is that it invariably dehumanizes some person or group of people and becomes a pretext for injustice. Socialism denies people the fruit of their labor, thus removing the natural incentive for work—which is a healthy and moral human activity. It separates people from the joy of earning their own sustenance, replacing it with dependence.

The record of socialism's "for the common good" mindset is dismal. In Germany, Adolph Hitler and his National Socialists directed the murder of 6 million, most of whom were Jews. Although Communism is but a subcategory of socialist systems, it alone accounts for an estimated 100 million deaths in the 20th century, a figure that does not include an estimated 400 million forced abortions by the regime in China during the period from the late-1970s through 2012.[8] Communist China leads in deaths in raw numbers—65 million—with the two largest massacres being the Great Famine (1959-1961)—caused by the Great Leap Forward, which killed about 50 million people—and the Cultural Revolution (1966-1976), with estimated deaths between 2 and 20 million. Mao Zedong presided over the entire period. The Soviet Union was responsible for the next highest death toll, 20 million. In Cambodia, Pol Pot killed an estimated 2-3 million of his

---

7. The NIV, ESV, and NASB contain this term nowhere else.
8. During this period, women who appeared pregnant without papers were hunted down, involuntarily transported to facilities, and forced to undergo the termination of their babies. Note that this figure alone is greater than the current total population of the United States. Xi Van Fleet, personal conversation, December 2, 2024.

people, which amounted to one-quarter to one-third of the country's population. In North Korea, the figure is 2 million. Communism in Vietnam, Latin America, Africa, Afghanistan, and Eastern Europe together killed another 5.35 million.[9]

WHY SOCIALISM FAILS

Socialism fails, first, because it systematizes injustice. It allows theft, and it rewards people for punishing a man if he does something to benefit society. The second proximal economic reason that socialism fails is that it does not account for human nature. In fact, it punishes activities that the Bible says are good, such as working to provide for oneself and one's family, engaging in commerce, seeking to earn a profit, and saving for the future.

In other words, socialism denies the natural structure that leads to prosperity as God designed it within the framework of six days of work followed by one day of rest. The happy effects of people diligently pursuing their own interests was the subject of Adam Smith's famous comment, "By promoting his own interest [the individual] frequently promotes that of the society more effectually than when he really intends to promote it."[10]

Socialists have failed to understand that biblical economic justice—which is today roughly identical to what we call capitalism—is the great engine of human prosperity because, first, it affirms what the Bible affirms. You shall not steal. If you need or want something that someone else owns, you must obtain it by gift or by purchase, not by theft. Second, you will most likely succeed

---

9. Stéphane Courtois et al., *The Black Book of Communism: Crimes, Terror, Repression* (Cambridge: Harvard University Press, 1999), 4. See also Victims of Communism Memorial Foundation. https://victimsof communism.org.

10. Adam Smith, *An Inquiry into the Nature and Causes of the Wealth of Nations*, Norwalk: Easton Press (1991), 347-8.

in obtaining it if you offer something the other person wants or needs in exchange. Now, you may be lazy or unskilled, but when you need or want something, you will apply the energies and talents that God gave you in order to get what you need.

The advances in science and medicine that have improved the lives of untold millions have primarily come into reality within a capitalist system, and far less frequently from within societies that have other systems. People in third-world countries today have extended lives, restored vision, relief from plague and pestilence, and improved public health due in part to the fruits that came into this world through the affirmation of liberty and property in the United States and elsewhere. These are advances that *would not exist* but for capitalism.[11]

Here is a partial list of what commonly happens under socialist governments: Corruption, loss of liberty, abuse of the innocent (including murder of categories of people), increased costs on goods and services, decreased quality, stunted and unequal opportunity (often based upon personal connections, and limited to a certain range of activities and outcomes), loss of accountable government, centralization of power, and inflation.

IS SOCIALISM CHRISTIAN?

Some Christians have come to believe that socialism is just, compassionate, and morally upright. Because the Bible calls for all three, and because God is love (1 John 4:8), they become warm to socialism. The flawed argument that convinces a few that socialism is what God wants—that those who don't support it are bad and selfish—goes something like this:

---

11. Abuses of power can arise under any economic system. Laws should be just, and they should be upheld by a judicial system that favors neither rich nor poor.

GOD TELLS ME TO CARE FOR THE POOR, *AND*
SOCIALISM HELPS THE POOR, *THEREFORE*
GOOD PEOPLE MUST SUPPORT SOCIALISM

But this argument contains at least two fatal flaws. First, the premise "socialism helps the poor" is mostly false. The poor actually suffer harm under socialism—see the examples of my cousin-in-law in Florida (Chapter 10), and Charlie Gard (above). But also, harm and injustice are perpetrated against many others under socialism, as bystanders become enslaved to their own plundering neighbors and society becomes callous and cold-hearted, since "care" for others is delegated to a government agency.

Second, the argument is a classic example of the *false choice* fallacy. It presents only two options—an obviously wrong one ("don't help the poor")—and a second that is less self-evidently bad to most people ("support socialism"). That is, it tells people that if they do not support socialism, then they must not want to help the poor. But it is possible to help the poor without doing injustice to them or to others—that is, without succumbing to socialism.

As has been stated, socialism rests upon an assertion that there is no natural right to property, that unequal wealth distribution is morally wrong, and that forced wealth redistribution by government is therefore just and desirable. Accordingly, socialists justify plunder through the democratic process—and eventually through an authoritarian one-party communist state. As has been demonstrated throughout this book, neither position aligns with God's word, the Bible. The core premise of capitalism is that life, liberty, and the pursuit of happiness are rights given to every human being by our Creator. In fact, no human right can exist apart from the existence of absolute truth and God.

A final theological reason that socialism cannot be considered Christian is that another of its fundamental premises is antithetical to the gospel of Jesus Christ itself. The belief that joy must be contingent upon material circumstances is a false assertion that destroys lives. If you postpone feeling joy and contentment until perfect justice is done in your life, let alone the world, you could wait a very long time. And if your ideal circumstances come, they will likely not last. In contrast Paul wrote of true liberation: "I have learned to be content in whatever circumstances I am. I know how to get along with humble means, and I also know how to live in prosperity; in any and every circumstance I have learned the secret of being filled and going hungry, both of having abundance and suffering need" (Philippians 4:11-12). And again, "godliness *actually* is a means of great gain when accompanied by contentment" (1 Timothy 6:6).

Culture, teachers, entertainers, friends, relatives—even a trusted pastor or church leader—may stand against what God says is good and right. That is why Paul gave specific individual instruction, in Romans 12:2, to not conform to the pattern of this world, but to be transformed by the renewing of our mind. According to Paul, renewing our mind is not automatic or passive; we must decide and act—otherwise, why would he have given the Romans such an instruction? James similarly wrote that an aspect of pure and faultless religion in God's eyes is to keep oneself unstained by the world (James 1:27).

CHAPTER 18

Who Wants Socialism

I n Chapter 1, we mentioned the general reason that people sometimes support socialism: politicians or bureaucrats interested in diminishing individual rights implement policies that over time impoverish enough people, making them willing to vote for more government "help." But there are, in fact, several types of people who like socialism, not all of them conniving.

SWEET POISON

If we poll the people of a socialist country, what might we find? Recent polls show that many people (though nowhere a majority) have a positive opinion of socialism. Unsurprisingly, young people who have not yet accumulated property tend to be socialism's biggest supporters. A 2023 study in the U.K. showed that 53 percent of respondents aged 18-34 said socialism is the ideal economic system.[1] A similar poll in Canada found that 50 percent of Canadians in this age category favor socialism—though

---

1. Jason Clemens and Steven Globerman, "New poll finds strong sup-

few want to be the ones paying for it.[2] In the United States, support for socialism among young people trended upward from 2010 through 2023,[3] though the trend in positive views of socialism in all age categories was level,[4] or downward.[5] But, what's the problem? If a growing minority likes it, then socialism must not be that terrible, right?

The *argumentum ad populum*, or "bandwagon fallacy," is a logical error which says that if lots of people support something, it must be good. We have many examples from history to demonstrate, however, that it is simply not true. Common sense tells us that even if *most* people in a society have a favorable view of cannibalism, it doesn't mean that everyone should stop caring about the poor guy who is on the menu for tomorrow night. In Chapter 2, we showed that the Bible says justice is owed to *everyone*, not just to those in the majority. Socialism is a system of widespread abuse, perpetrated against the defenseless minority. Half of society gang up on the wealthy and make them pay for everyone else's wants and needs. Indeed, the wealthy are also forced to pay for waste, since government has never run anything more efficiently than its private free-market counterpart would have done.

Self-interest and youthful ignorance do not entirely account for the elevated levels of support for socialism among younger people. Remember that socialism is an

port for socialism in the U.K." *Fraser Institute*. March 24, 2023. (December 3, 2024).

2. Jason Clemens and Steven Globerman, "New poll reveals 50% of Canadians 18-24 favour socialism, but few Canadians willing to pay for it." *Fraser Institute*. February 23, 2023. (December 3, 2024).

3. Jason Clemens and Steven Globerman, *Perspectives on Capitalism and Socialism: Polling Results from Canada, the United States, Australia, and the United Kingdom* (Fraser Institute, 2023).

4. Frank Newport, "Public Opinion Review: Americans' Reactions to the Word 'Socialism'" *Gallup*, March 6, 2020.

5. Pew Research Center, "Modest Declines in Positive Views of 'Socialism' and 'Capitalism' in U.S." September 2022.

authoritarian ideology that dominates by force in the name of the "greater good." Socialist states usually have a highly centralized education system that teaches children according to the reigning government orthodoxy. Children who grow up learning that wealth inequality is unjust and that government should run everything are likely to continue holding such views when they become adults.

We turn now to a fuller discussion of who supports socialism. Generally, I propose that socialism's supporters fall into two categories: *self-serving scoundrels*, and *otherwise decent people who have been duped*. Let's proceed.

WHAT PEOPLE LIKE ABOUT SOCIALISM

As the above-referenced polls demonstrate, socialism is not disliked by everyone. However, among those who do approve of it, only a portion are otherwise decent dupes. Envy, hate, greed, and fear are the main emotions that activists tap into when trying to persuade constituents to vote for socialist politicians and policies. Socialism tends to be popular among those who are not paying into it, or who at least figure they will get more out than they put in. Such people may soothe their consciences by demonizing those who pay, asserting they "can afford it," they should pay their "fair share," or that it is only right that they foot the bill since "society has been so good to them."

Let's turn now to our general types. To be clear, I do *not* apply every one of the following descriptions to every socialist. And, please remember that everyone, including the scoundrel, is made in God's image and—more than anything—needs to hear and respond to the gospel.

DUPES

Some people honestly believe that socialism is good, or at the very least that it does not really hurt anyone—and that by supporting it, they are doing a good thing. They may have been raised to believe that the "greater good" is sufficient reason to deny justice to some individuals or, if they were not raised that way, they may have been led to such belief by teachers or professors. When the hundred million dead from socialism in the past century are mentioned to them, they may reply that those governments were not practicing *real* socialism, or that socialism simply hasn't been done the right way yet.

Weak ideas often gain acceptance through appeal to faulty arguments and empty slogans. One common fallacy is circular reasoning, an example of which I noticed recently. The subheadline on a pro-socialist article hosted by NBC News proclaimed, "The next generation of socialists believes that the intolerable cannot be tolerated."[6] *Wow*, I said to myself, *it sure is good to know that young socialists understand that a thing is equal to itself.* Now, that ridiculous heading went in circles, but some people will not notice. Rather, they may be moved, and perhaps think, "Hey, that's right! We're not going to take it any more! I'm glad those socialists won't put up with the intolerable!"

Misdirection distracts from reality, hiding the truth by diversion. Used by a magician, misdirection draws attention away from the natural explanation, causing one to be mystified and to perceive that the magician has defied the laws of nature. It is not immoral to use misdirection for entertainment, when there is an implicit agreement between deceiver and deceived. When used by thieves or dishonest politicians to plunder unwitting victims or cause people to lend support to some bad action or policy, however, misdirection becomes an instrument of injustice. Protecting the guilty, harming the innocent, or leading people to victimize others—none of these is good.

---

6. Nathan J. Robinson, "Millennials support socialism because they want to make America great—but for everyone," NBC News, January 1, 2020.

Defenders of all kinds of evil commonly distract by misnaming things, or by pointing a finger of blame at the innocent as a means of distraction. Some flag words that socialist politicians often employ to trick dupes into going along with socialist policies include "fair," "affordable," "social justice," "liberation," "victim," "privilege," "inequality," "access," "dignity," "affordable," and "attainable." Meanwhile, they accuse their critics of being opposed to taxation, to fairness, to clean air and water, of being "anti-worker," or of wanting children to starve. Since this book is primarily an evaluation of socialism, there is no need to engage in a lengthy discussion of the word tricks used by Marxists, but one passage from the Bible will serve to illustrate the origin of their technique:

> Then the Lord God took the man and put him into the garden of Eden to cultivate it and keep it. The Lord God commanded the man, saying, "From any tree of the garden you may eat freely; but from the tree of the knowledge of good and evil you shall not eat, for in the day that you eat from it you will surely die." [...]

> Now the serpent was more crafty than any beast of the field which the Lord God had made. And he said to the woman, "Indeed, has God said, 'You shall not eat from any tree of the garden'?" The woman said to the serpent, "From the fruit of the trees of the garden we may eat; but from the fruit of the tree which is in the middle of the garden, God has said, 'You shall not eat from it or touch it, or you will die.'" The serpent said to the woman, "You surely will not die! For God knows that in the day you eat from it your eyes will be opened, and you will be like God, knowing good and evil." When the woman saw that the tree was good for food, and that it was a delight to the eyes, and that the tree was desirable to make *one* wise, she took from its fruit and ate; and she gave also to her

husband with her, and he ate. (Genesis 2:15-17; 3:1-6)

The detail to observe is that, first, when the serpent spoke to the woman, he *immediately* began twisting God's words. God had given Adam and Eve freedom to eat from *every* tree in this beautiful garden, except for one. But the serpent began by asking, "Indeed, has God said, 'You shall not eat from any tree of the garden'?" It was a lie, and the serpent twisted God's kindness to make Him look stingy. And, notice Eve follows suit by adding a prohibition, "or touch it," that God had never spoken. And we see the rest of the tragedy. After the serpent craftily planted a seed of doubt concerning God's good intentions for Adam and Eve in Eve's mind, that seed quickly grew into the bitter fruit of sin and death.

In the category of dupes who have been tricked into thinking that support for socialism is benign, there are also successful people with sizeable incomes. These individuals often feel that they are demonstrating love for the poor by voting for socialism. They may feel as though they would be guilty of insensitivity if they were to vote against the growth of government programs or redistribution efforts—and they sometimes enjoy a sense of redemption, even enlightened superiority, when they vote for socialist programs. Some of these people, unfortunately, look down upon those who do not do so, considering them uncompassionate, insensitive, or selfish.

SOME WHO ARE DISCOURAGED, HOPELESS, AND BROKEN

Although not all of us will wind up supporting socialism, feelings of of deep discouragement, hopelessness, and brokenness are part of being human, and describe most of us at some point in life. Many experience such circumstances many times. Some people endure a heavy trial for years, even a lifetime. For those who have been broken by trauma, the effects can linger for a very long time.

And then there are those who feel they've tried everything, who perhaps even feel they've messed up their lives beyond repair, and are tempted to give up hope. Such people may conclude that they have no choice but to lay their burden upon the rest of society, the shoulders of those who—to them—look more stable and secure. If this scenario describes you, first let me say I empathize with your heartache, your experience of actual betrayal or injustice at the hands of another or others, or whatever else you have been through or are going through right now. Second, may I encourage you that God will take care of you, even through circumstances that you feel could not possibly be worse (James 1:2-4; Romans 8:28). There is hope. God sees. You do not know what tomorrow will bring. But I assure you that your future will be better if you choose to trust God and do whatever you know is right.

Someone who perceives that he has few prospects for advancement, or who senses that life has not been fair, may choose to support a system that promises to help him personally, add a sense of security, and calm his worries about the future. He may be willing to sacrifice something vague and abstract like *liberty* for something that feels more tangible, like *security*. Sure, his life may be modest, taxes higher, and opportunities for success limited. Given his current situation, he is fine with that. Thoughts of justice and human rights for those who will be victimized by socialism seem abstract and distant to many people in these situations, while their own problems are immediate and frightening.

POWERFUL AND EVIL MEN

Now we come to the scoundrels, and the first of three categories contains those with an insatiable greed for money who have determined that harnessing the coercive power of government will best serve their own business aspirations. Contrary to popular belief, socialism is not principally powered by true concern for the poor or the downtrodden. As you saw in the example of Nathan in Chapter 10, socialism is *big business*, and it trades in money and power. Poor and suffering people are merely props that serve as the ongoing pretext for the enrichment and empowerment of the socialist cronies.

Socialism enriches and empowers a certain type of man. He is not the rugged individualist businessman. No, he is the George Soros and Klaus Schwab type, the sort of Bond-villain who pushes for "public-private partnership" and somehow rakes in millions or billions over the course of his "service" to humanity.

An old communist slogan that was revived by Barack Obama in 2012 and later picked up by Kamala Harris is "Forward."[7] It leapfrogs over questions of where "forward" leads. Green pastures are different from swimming pools filled with shards of broken glass, and which destination lies ahead would seem an important detail when charting a course. The counterpart of this statement was repeated in Harris' short-lived 2024 presidential campaign, when she defiantly announced, "We are *not* going back!" Harris, who came by the nomination without having to win popular support, was the most openly and ideologically socialist presidential candidate in American history.[8]

7. Victor Morton, "New Obama slogan has long ties to Marxism, socialism," *The Washington Times*, April 30, 2012.
8. Merrill Matthews, "Harris's agenda mirrors the Democratic Socialists of America," *The Hill*, September 24, 2024.

SELF-RIGHTEOUS SHIRKERS OF MORAL DUTY

Identifying human need is not difficult. One can hardly drive a mile or walk a few city blocks without encountering someone who needs help. We cannot individually solve all the problems of every person we meet, nor are we obligated to do so. Remember, we are not our brother's keeper; we owe our brothers and sisters *justice* (i.e., fairness before the law) and *mercy* (personal kindness and love). And, Jesus' basic instruction was actually quite simple: "Give to everyone who asks of you" (Luke 6:30). Ideally, you and I should give *something* to everyone who asks for help, and we should treat it as a special moral imperative if we encounter someone in a life-threatening situation.

Statistically, Americans are the most generous people in the world,[9] and "practicing Christians" are far and away the most generous Americans.[10] We are used to tithing and to holding our money lightly. Most Christians are not socialists and most socialists are not Christians. Many socialists are people who act as though caring for the needy is *someone else's job*. These are people who seemingly can't be bothered to take personal action by way of meaningful financial contribution, so they vote to force other people to deal with the poor.

THE LAZY, COVETOUS, OR OTHERWISE MORALLY DEPRAVED

It is easy to look at a successful person and imagine that she had it easy. But more often than not, there was a lot of

---

9. Leslie Albrecht, "The U.S. is the No. 1 most generous country in the world for the last decade," *Market Watch*, December 7, 2019.
10. Ryan Foley, "Practicing Christians give more to charity than non-Christians: study," *The Christian Post*, November 15, 2023.

discipline, self-denial, delayed gratification, and pure hard work that preceded anyone's success story. It is common to see a person doing well and wonder why it's not you. In the midst of success stories everywhere, the socialist whispers: *She didn't earn it ... she's "privileged." She doesn't deserve so much. She doesn't need so much. She probably does not pay her fair share. She should.*

Such messages hit home in the ear of those quick to blame and slow to take personal responsibility. These are people with bitter hearts and chips on their shoulders, who want results without hardship, uncertainty, or self-sacrifice. Such people are easily tempted to embrace thievery and injustice as a shortcut to wealth and security.

CHAPTER SUMMARY

Supporters of socialism fall generally into two categories: Self-serving scoundrels, and well-meaning people who have been duped. The tricks and manipulations of the former are one reason for the existence of the latter. Socialism is an enormous global business flowing with ill-gotten money and power, and this business continues to line the pockets of those in control so long as those receiving handouts do not become self-sufficient.

CHAPTER 19

Love Must Be Sincere

A 12-year-old boy sat down on his bed in Madrid, Spain in early 1983 to read six chapters of his Bible, starting in Genesis, then did the same the next day, and the next. He had become a Christian at age 5, but now, as a kid on the verge of adulthood, he wanted to read God's entire word for himself. That boy was me. I finished Revelation the day we moved back to the United States in 1984.

Anyone can read through the Bible. Everyone *should* do it. *You* should do it. But over the years, I have learned that most people—even many of those who have attended church alongside us for many years—never *have* done it.

There are lots of good reasons to know your Bible. Much of the society you live in has been shaped by it and refers to it, so if you know what it says, you will have an advantage in life. More importantly, the Bible contains God's words to us, telling us how to be saved and giving wisdom for living. You may not yet believe it to be true, and that's all right. Regardless of what anyone believes it to be, when one makes a claim about what the Bible says, that claim ought to be based on knowledge of its text, and the only real way to gain such knowledge is to *read the Bible*.

Many people, if they read it at all, take only occasional brief dives into the text, grabbing what they want, and returning to the surface with little or no context. Sometimes they do it in pursuit of a specific outcome, maybe to show that God *really* supports this, or that He *really* does not condemn that. Then, free from the constraints of the rest of scripture, they make these snippets say what they wish. Through such maneuvering, the word of God becomes a mere prop in the hands of people who don't really care what God wants, people who in some cases don't even believe He exists.

THE END OF THE MATTER

We have covered a lot of ground in this book, but we've only scratched the surface of the treasures you can find inside the Bible. This book has been a *topical* study, meaning it is an attempt to survey the Bible for answers on a specific question, rather than the other common method of biblical exploration, called *expository*, which begins with a passage rather than a topic. Both types of study should involve *exegesis*. Exegesis means taking out and faithfully presenting—discovering—what the Author of the text is saying, rather than trying to hijack the text to make it support some other message that may not have ever been intended (that would be called *eisegesis*, and it is not a good way to approach the Bible). During this study, I've tried to minimize repetition, and to avoid belaboring the points. I did not want to weary you by citing too many scriptures or going into too much detail—but I also wanted you to feel the weight of these many references, for you to know that they exist.

If you've read the Bible through, and maybe even done so multiple times, I expect you've discovered (as have I) that, while it is full of and overflowing with details that could be explored over many lifetimes, and while its 66 books contain great variety and were written by multiple different authors in disparate times and places and circumstances, it also tells a consistent and unified story.

The unified story of the Bible, as mentioned in Chapter 3, is that of God's love and provision for mankind, whom He created in His own image for the purpose of loving relationship with Him. Since sin entered the world through Adam and Eve, the Bible also tells the story of God's kind redemption (rescue) of those who were lost—you and me. The life ring by which we can be saved—the only one (Acts 4:12)—is Jesus Christ, Who made payment for all the sins of any who will trust Him. We grab onto this life ring by believing in His name (John 1:12), but the saving work is not our own—it is God's (Ephesians 2:8-9).

Considering the vast size and beauty of the universe, some people may think it ridiculous to assert that the purpose of God's creation could be so focused upon concern for individual human beings, tiny creatures on a small planet, the entirety of which is a miniscule speck among trillions upon trillions of stars and galaxies spanning unimaginable distances whose end has not yet been discerned. Of course, these are deep matters that we could ponder and discuss at great length. But if the Bible is God's word, then we have direct testimony from God Himself that this is in fact the case.

The topic of this book, really, concerns a big question about what real justice means in our relationship with other people. The prevailing culture today—sometimes called the "spirit of the age"—says that justice among humans requires equality of material outcome, regardless of all other factors, and that this equality should be adjudicated and enforced by some human governing authority.

As I have argued in this book, the Bible sharply disagrees with the spirit of the age on this subject. It affirms both justice and mercy, while clearly defining what those terms mean. Biblical justice includes the affirmation of property and a corresponding prohibition of theft and coveting—as well as affirmation that differing pay rates (based upon mutual agreement between parties) and differing wealth levels are *just*.

So, what is the end of the matter for us, concerning socialism? There are several ways we might put it, but combining a statement of Jesus with the words of the prophet Micah, let us wrap things up like this:

> Love the LORD your God, and love your neighbor as yourself (Matthew 22:36-40). Doing so will cause you to do justice, love mercy, and walk humbly with your God (Micah 6:8). Loving God and walking humbly with Him will mean keeping His commandments (John 14:15), and agreeing with Him (rather than with the world) about what is right and what is wrong, loving what He loves and hating what He hates.

This book's title emphasizes my contention that socialism (as defined in Chapter 1) is *wrong*, and that although Christians might support it, they cannot do so without turning their backs on God's commands. I have presented throughout this book, from the Bible, why I believe this to be the case. Of course, just as there are Christians who are adulterers and murderers,[1] so also there do exist Christians who support socialism—if they have trusted Jesus for the forgiveness of their sins, they are saved and will be with us in heaven. I've never heard of a person who forever stopped sinning after following Jesus. And in dealing with each other, we should remember the

---

1. And before any of us who have not committed literal adultery or fornication or murder get too comfortable, we are reminded of Jesus' words, "I say to you that everyone who looks at a woman with lust for her has already committed adultery with her in his heart" (Matthew 5:28), and "everyone who is angry with his brother shall be guilty before the court [i.e., of murder]" (Matthew 5:22).

grace that we ourselves receive from God: "For by grace you have been saved through faith; and that not of your-selves, *it is* the gift of God; not as a result of works, so that no one may boast" (Ephesians 2:8-9).

We all have rough edges and hard hearts that soften and shine more brightly over time as we allow ourselves to be in the presence of Jesus. When Moses came down from the mountain after spending time with God, his face was so bright that he had to wear a veil (Exodus 34:29-30). In similar fashion, our lives shine more as we spend time in the presence of Jesus. "But the path of the righteous is like the light of dawn, that shines brighter and brighter until the full day" (Proverbs 4:18). In one of the most moving analogies I know, the late musician Keith Green likened people to stained glass windows whose full beauty is only revealed when the Son shines through.[2]

I hope it has become clear as we've walked through the scriptures together that socialism does not align with justice, and that you should not, therefore, embrace or advocate for it. Thank you for reading.

2. Green, Keith, and Melody Green. "Stained Glass." Track 9 on *No Compromise*. Sparrow, 1978, vinyl.

Appendix: About Liberation Theology

Liberation theologies are theological systems that change the people, words, and stories of the Bible to support radical egalitarian materialism, also known as Marxism.

Clues that a system may be liberation theology instead of biblical theology include its prominent use of terms like "social justice," "oppression," "liberation," "violence," "victimization," "class," "privilege," "struggle," "fight," "inequality," "access," "solidarity," "dignity," "poverty," "structural" or "institutional" (e.g., poverty, racism, etc.), "affordable" or "attainable" (e.g., housing, healthcare, etc.), or "scandal" (e.g., of poverty, of inequality, etc.)—all of which permeate Marxism while not being central terms or concepts in biblical theology.

Liberation theology grew in the halls of academia during the latter part of the twentieth century as part of a strategy by Marxists to overcome their "Christian problem." Marxism has only three options when it comes to biblical Christianity:

1. Dominate or destroy its adherents
2. Be destroyed by it

3. Tame it by making it seem to support Marxism

Although the first option was commonly practiced in the 20th century,[1] the third option has also been embraced, and it has manifested in such forms as the Chinese Three Self Church and in the growth of liberation theologies. This last has proven quite effective for the advance of Marxism in Western Europe, the United States and Canada, Latin America, and sub-Saharan Africa.

Actual past and present injustices fueled the emergence and popular appeal of liberation theologies. However, the overlay of Marxian thought, subordinating everything to a radical materialist reduction of human relationships to a binary and rigid system of oppressor versus oppressed, rich versus poor, advantaged versus disadvantaged, the powerful versus the powerless, is what makes liberation theologies mostly irreconcilable with the Bible. In direct defiance of Leviticus 19:15 and other scriptural mandates such as Exodus 23:3, liberation theologies tend to represent those designated oppressors, advantaged, rich, or powerful as less deserving—or even undeserving—of justice.

Liberation theologies' general rejection of property also makes them hostile to biblical justice. Indeed, Marxism's divorce of justice from labor and its fruits and its low view of human worth, as well as liberation theologians' preference for biblical eisegesis rooted in grievance and human vengeance rather than grace and hope grounded in biblical justice, cause these systems to perpetrate injustice rather than alleviate it. Often the result is more grievous than the problems they purport to address.

Liberation theology is activist by nature and is aligned

---

1. Many of the more than 100 million singled out for execution by Communists have been Christians, including pastors, scholars, teachers, and evangelists.

with leftist or revolutionary politics in the United States and abroad. Today, liberation theology is used to attach a façade of biblical respectability to the identity politics of socialist and Marxist feminism, LGBTQ+ movements, open borders advocacy, socialism, labor unions, abortion-on-demand, environmental causes that spiritualize nature and elevate plants and animals above humanity, multiculturalism, totalitarianism (including fascist organizations like Antifa with its violent and heavy-handed tactics), and similar movements.

HISTORY

Liberation theology emerged by name in the latter part of the 20th century, but it is part of older spiritual, social, political, and intellectual trends. Important areas of emergence and development in the last half-century have included Latin America, the Catholic Church, and the American (and British) Left, particularly in theologically liberal churches and seminaries (i.e., ones that have a low view of scripture).

The modern basis for liberation theology was laid in the ethos of the French Revolution. Liberation theology in most of its manifestations runs contrary to two foundational principles of the American declaration of "liberty and justice for all": 1) the American (and biblical) recognition that property (i.e., the fruit of human labor) is a necessary precondition to both liberty and justice, and 2) the American (and biblical) affirmation of equality among human beings and that justice shows no favoritism. Both are generally rejected by liberation theologies.

Concurrent with the work of abolitionists to lift the United States up to these two principles that undergird the Declaration of Independence's assertion that life, liberty, and the pursuit of happiness are the natural rights of every human being, an alternate groundwork was being laid by materialist public intellectuals of the late 19th

Century within the United States based on the proposition that rights are socially constructed rather than universal. These ideas found fertile soil in the self-serving moral relativism of the defeated South at the end of the Civil War and achieved key footholds in American government with the passage of the 16th and 17th Amendments to the U.S. Constitution, making possible the implementation of FDR's Great Society. Though the movement was not new, the term "liberation theology" itself was coined by Gustavo Gutierrez in 1971, and quickly came to describe a school of theologians sharing these premises.

Liberation theology is "theology" because it makes claims about God. However, it rests upon views of justice, the nature of reality, and the nature of mankind that are foreign to the Old and New Testaments but embraced and advanced by political philosophers including Plato, Emmanuel Kant, G.W.F. Hegel, Karl Marx, Martin Heidegger, Jacques Derrida, and others. Liberation theology has become the preferred and dominant paradigm among governing and academic elites around the world, including the United Nations, all of whom prefer to see rights as politically determined and originating with human institutions.

As liberation theologies leverage the concepts of "victim" and "oppressor" toward political revolution, the elusive nature of material equality ensures the impossibility of actual resolution. This circumstance creates ongoing political advantage for individuals who benefit from grievance, such as politicians who promise to redistribute wealth, or union bosses who pocket millions on the backs of the laborers they "protect." Salvation, thus, is made contingent upon absolute material equity and placed eternally out of reach for every human being, who is then invited to instead nurse a lifelong hatred and resentment of others who fit into some part of the "oppressor" category. Liberation theologies, because rooted in materialism and

Marxism's low view of human worth, often justify violence up to and including mass murder, so long as the ones being harmed are defined as "oppressors."

CATHOLIC CHURCH AND CATHOLIC SOCIAL TEACHING

In May of 1891, Pope Leo XIII issued the encyclical *Rerum Novarum*. The document on the one hand affirms the right to property and rejects socialism as injustice. However, it is also saturated with Marxist jargon and categories. The terms "class(es)" and "the working class(es)" occur 32 times in the space of 20 pages, and the document uses the term "proletarian" as well as referring to the apparent oxymoron "unchecked competition."

The *Rerum Novarum* contains the seeds of what later came to be known as the "preferential option for the poor" when it claims that "when there is question of defending the rights of individuals, the poor and badly off have a claim to especial consideration." The statement seems to intend counterbalancing the advantages of rich people via an imposed counter advantage to poor or weak people. However, here it countermands biblical justice, which says that neither rich nor poor should be shown favoritism, but everyone should be judged fairly (Leviticus 19:15).

The *Rerum Novarum,* though correctly defending property as essential to justice, nevertheless cracked open the door to both injustice and socialism, when it declared, "the public administration must duly and solicitously provide for the welfare and the comfort of the working classes," and "Justice ... demands that the interests of the working classes should be carefully watched over by the administration," and other such statements. The *Rerum Novarum's* error at these points laid a foundation for the Catholic Church's subsequent dalliance with liberation theology.

Having gained a foothold in the Latin American Catholic Church throughout the 1960s and 1970s, Marxism eventually bore fruit in the form of a bona fide socialist Pope, Francis. Douglas Farrow opened his 2017 article in the Catholic magazine *First Things*, "'Is the pope Catholic?' used to be an answer, not a question."[2] The reference here is not merely to Francis' embrace of liberation theology, but also to his slack and apparently compromising stance toward moral matters that, scripturally speaking, are non-negotiable.

OTHER LIBERATION THEOLOGIES

The Peruvian Gustavo Gutiérrez began using the term "theology of liberation" in the late 1960s. In 1971, John Rawls published his extensive book *A Theory of Justice*, which redefined justice using Marxian terms (e.g., "distributive justice") and became the cornerstone of subsequent social justice activism in the West that continues to this day. James Cone is the father of Black liberation theology. Feminist and Womanist liberation theologies have also been important, as have been Latin American and Third-World liberation theologies, the latter being heavily intertwined with the Catholic Church.

SUMMARY

Christian theologies vary on many points, but all affirm certain core propositions: 1) God is neither myth nor invention, but exists eternally apart from His temporal creation, 2) God has spoken, 3) God created all men and women in His own image and gave them dominion over the earth, 4) The Hebrew Bible and New Testament in their original languages constitute God's inerrant revela-

---

2. Douglas Farrow, "Discernment of situation," *First Things*, March 2017.

5) Jesus was no mere man, but the Word Who was with God and was God in the beginning, His death and resurrection being the only possible atonement for sin, effective for all who take refuge in it, 6) Justice is to be sought, but joy in this life is not contingent upon material circumstances. Most liberation theologians deny, overtly or implicitly, one or more of the above six propositions. In most cases, liberation theology is thus not Christian theology.

Many liberation theologians, indeed, are skeptical concerning the authority of the Bible, and even sometimes about the existence of God. Some are admitted atheists. The actual existence of an unseen spiritual universe that is as real as the material world, however—including a God Who judges, Who sees the poor and oppressed, and Who will surely address every wrong—are solid and explicit givens of the Hebrew Bible and the New Testament. Liberation theologians in general would do well to return to the biblical instruction: "Do not be overcome by evil, but overcome evil with good" (Romans 12:21) and Jesus' instruction to pray for those who persecute you and bless those who curse you (Matthew 5:44).

Perhaps the greatest irony of liberation theology is its name. The heart of the gospel is that people can be free from slavery to sin, totally forgiven: "So if the Son makes you free, you will be free indeed" (John 8:36, see also Psalm 147:3 and Isaiah 61:1). This statement is not contingent upon one's material situation but only upon Jesus Himself. Liberation theologies put joy perpetually out of reach, dependent upon a societal situation that is humanly impossible and therefore will never exist. Such grievance helps the political advocates of revolution, but it deadens the human spirit and denies the joy that Jesus makes available in even the worst circumstance.

Liberation theology, in summary, is a Marxist project to infiltrate and neutralize Christians, to condition them to prefer Marxist theology over biblical theology by tricking them into believing that the former *is*, in fact, the latter. The purpose of liberation theology is to persuade Christians to abandon a sound biblical view of the world and of their neighbors.

Index of Scripture References